MW00674688

Birds, Buffaloes, and Birthday Bread

Stories of Redemption and Rest
for the Weary Traveler

Andrew M. Lepper

Copyright @ 2016 by Andrew M Lepper

All rights reserved. No part of this book may be reproduced
in any form by any electronic or mechanical means including
information storage or retrieval systems — for example,
electronic, photocopy, recording — without the prior written
permission of the author. The only exception is brief
quotations in printed reviews.

To protect the privacy of those referenced in this book, in
most cases names, locations, and details have been changed.

Cover design @ 2016 by Scott Cuzzo
www.scottcuzzo.com

Cover images @ 2016 by Andy Lepper

"Do you wonder what really happens in world missions? Have you ever wondered if lives are actually changed? Andy's book will give you a glimpse into the real world of those dedicated to serving others. His stories will remove any doubt about the power of God's love to change lives, and touch your heart in the process."

- Mike Loomis, Writer and Coach

"If you are looking for a book that will both give you perspective regarding the blessings in your life and give you hope that a difference can be made in the lives of those less fortunate, you have found that book. This book is packed with real stories of changed lives."

- Randy Langley; www.LaunchOut.com

"Andy takes us on a delightful and realistic journey into a very real India - a place far removed, and in many ways more beautiful - than the exotic country displayed so often in travel magazines. His stories reveal what we all have in common - a longing for family, a desire for a place to call home, and the impact we can all have to change lives for the better through the simple act of saying "yes" to God's heart for the orphan."

- Ronne Rock
writer | speaker | advocate | adventurer

"I thought I knew what crazy faith was until I met Andy Lepper and his wife, Susan. What they are doing in India for orphan boys blew my mind. It is a lifestyle of faith that few of us have experienced. This powerful book will so inspire you. I am fortunate I got to witness firsthand the life of the man who wrote it."

-John Waller
Singer-Songwriter, author,
owner of Crazy Faith Coffee Company

This book is dedicated to Mike and Lynn
for teaching me how to love,
and to Susan, Micah, and Joshua
for the chance every day to share that love.

Introduction

In order to fully understand this book, you need a little background about how it came into being. Andy is the Founder and President of No Longer Orphans, although he prefers the title of Chief Servant. No Longer Orphans exists to provide orphans with shelter, sustenance, education, and love so they may, in turn, impact their world for the glory of God. No Longer Orphans is the sole supporter of the Shiloh Children's Home located in North India and houses over forty orphans, all boys, ages four to eighteen. There is great potential for growth. The name "Shiloh" is a Hebrew word meaning "a place of rest for weary travelers." There are currently four guest rooms that can accommodate weary travelers as they serve the orphans. Before No Longer Orphans inherited the orphanage, the monthly food budget was less than $175. This allowed the children to have rice every day, but little to no meat or vegetables. No Longer Orphans has improved and will continue to improve the current state of the orphanage.

There are some bright sides to the story. Andy and Susan currently oversee the orphanage. They love the boys wholeheartedly and do an amazing job of teaching and holding them accountable. The boys love school and sports. They are vibrant and sing at the top of their lungs. No Longer Orphans is excited beyond words at the chance to serve the Shiloh Children's Home.

This book is a collection of Andy's blog posts about the children's home over the last three years. It has been compiled as it was written - chronologically. Due to this format, there may seem to be inconsistencies, but that is because of the natural growth and progression of the orphanage. On any page, you get a snapshot of the home at that given time. The numbers of boys, staff, and animals are constantly changing and is recorded as such in the story's entirety. What doesn't change is God's faithfulness and grace. As you read the account of our lives these last few years, our hope is that you will be encouraged and strengthened in your own faith. As you read some of the hardships and struggles of the boys, we pray that you will draw closer to God because He only is the author and perfect or of our faith. Don't feel bad for us. Don't take pity on our boys for their hard lives up till now. Join with us in thanking God that He continues to provide and also pray that we continue to serve Him with everything we have.

Amos the Brave (published on 09.25.13)

I truly love the boys with all my heart. Sometimes there are special moments with individuals you really treasure. I really enjoy all the little moments I get to spend with Amos. He is a firecracker, seven years old, and always going. His life has been pretty rough. Growing up, their mother was handicapped and their father was alcoholic, wasting away most of the family's money. He and his brother Ronnie came to the home two years ago when their father passed away from illness and their mother couldn't take care of them due to her condition.

Amos was super shy at first. He didn't know how to cope with the loss of his father, missing his mother, or all the new boys. But today, he is super lively and jokes all the time. He and his brother were the first to call me Papa, and get angry when the other boys call me something different.

One of the songs I taught the boys is "10,000 Reasons". It is an awesome worship song with the lines, "Bless the Lord, oh my soul. Oh, my soul. Worship your holy name." Amos loves this chorus and although he doesn't know the full song, not an hour goes by in the day where you can't hear him singing "bless the Lord" somewhere on our property.

I have only had two instances of crying the whole time I have been living at Shiloh with the twenty-eight boys. Amos was the first. I distributed to each of the boys thick rubber bouncy balls which were donated by a family from my church. They were heavy, bouncy, and built to last. Within five minutes of passing out the rubber balls, Amos ran into the path of one in motion and took it right in the eye. His eye immediately turned black and swelled shut. I was a nervous wreck. We immediately took him by motorcycle to the closest hospital where they told us there was little damage and that the swelling would go down. I was only able to get one photo of him without the black eye. Even through all of this, he barely cried, but he was the first boy to cry. I think he was in shock. Coincidentally, the other case of crying was his brother, Ronnie, who was crying because he was scared his brother's eye would fall out. Ha ha!

Amos had to miss one day of school and passed the day away by singing and playing on my IPad. Amos LOVES the game of cricket and I always have a willing partner who wants to play catch. He is just like me in that he HATES soccer, or futbol, or whatever it's called throughout the world. When all the boys want to play their daily, epic game of soccer, Amos can be found by my side, sitting under our favorite tree, sipping water, eating candy, and laughing at all the boys who think they know how to really play futbol, barefoot and all.

Saturday nights with Bruce Lee (published on 09.30.13)

When I was left the orphanage to travel in late January, I asked the boys what they wanted me to bring them back from the United States. They were very conservative and shy. One boy finally said, "a rubber ball." I told him I would surely do that, but I also encouraged them to ask for more. Two of the boys said, "Papa, we want chicken." I told them, "Of course, but tell me something more." After a few seconds, Roman raised his hand and proudly said, "Papa, bring ME one LCD flat screen television." I chuckled hard and told him I would try to make it happen, but it would be shared with everyone.

Fast forward to August. I had been so busy trying to provide the basic necessities that I forgot to purchase the television. So, for their birthday party, I bought them a flat screen. I brought a bunch of movies from the United States and asked them which one they would like to watch. They all started chanting, "Jackie Chan! Jackie Chan! Jackie Chan!" The problem was I had misplaced my two Jackie Chan movies, so I told them I had something better. I had a Bruce Lee movie! They had no idea who he was. I told them that Bruce Lee was like the father of

Jackie Chan. I put in the movie and they were silent. Their mouths were wide open for most of the movie. They were enthralled! Afterwards, a few boys told me that Bruce Lee was now their favorite action star.

For the next few days, they mimicked all the moves. Whenever we would have movie night, they only wanted to watch Bruce Lee. After the fifth viewing, I could take no more, so we started watching Bollywood movies which they also love. I found some popcorn we could heat on the stove. It became a weekly event on Saturday nights to watch Bollywood movies followed by Bruce Lee, all the while munching on popcorn and candy.

Everything in moderation...the boys' schedules are so full during the week that TV is a distraction. Between having school Monday to Saturday, they have chores and truly enjoy playing outside. My rule is no TV until Saturday afternoon. They really look forward to this time. Between the popcorn and the candy, it's one of the highlights of their week, not to mention Bruce Lee.

Crops We Grow; 10-3-13

We have the awesome privilege to enjoy living on twenty acres of land. Five of these acres are used for our building, driveway, and soccer field, leaving us with fifteen acres of agricultural land. We have two weather dynamics in our area. We have the highest recorded temperature in India at one hundred twenty-five degrees, but because of the monsoon season, we get a lot of rain in a short period of time. We have a similar average rainfall to Raleigh, North Carolina, although we have desert-like climate for ten months of the year. This quandary allows us to have plenty of well water but dry crops for most of the year, therefore, we are limited in what we plant and grow on the land.

Currently we grow corn, wheat, mustard, bajra, corn, and guar. Guar is a very important crop because it is used in the oil industry, making it a very beneficial and prosperous crop to grow. It is a volatile crop so it is hard to grow at times. Most of the time we grow the corn, wheat, and mustard.

We are able to mill mustard into oil, and the wheat and corn into flour. This helps us sustain the orphans, however, because of the low cost of the crops, we do not make enough in the marketplace. Our hope is to convert two to three acres into a large garden that the boys can cultivate. With more attention, we will be able to grow onions, tomatoes, beans, okra, and watermelons, just to name a few. We also want to have animals such as water buffaloes, goats, and chickens roaming free on our land. We will primarily use the animals for their milk and eggs. We give God the glory that we have this awesome amount of land to work with. Please join with us in prayer that one day the land will be able to better sustain us.

Reagan's Last Laugh (published on 10.08.13)

This is a simple post to let you know of our amazing laugher. I say this with no reservation, Reagan has the greatest laugh in the whole world. He is always laughing. Many times, I have stood in the middle of the building, closed my eyes and listened to hear where the boys may be on our property. Sometimes they are on the roof, sometimes there in the back field flying kites. Sometimes they are up front playing soccer. No matter where they are, when I close my eyes, I listen for Reagan's laugh. He never fails me. I can hear his boisterous laughter no matter where they are.

Reagan's laughter can melt the hardest of hearts. One day, I was joking with my orphanage coordinator that I wanted to have an award ceremony at the home soon. I said we would give prizes and awards based on how the boys behaved. There would be an award for the cleanest, the best student, etc. Vince said that the first award should go to Reagan for the best laugh, and I couldn't agree more. I asked the boys who were standing around who has the best laugh, and they all agree that it is Reagan.

Reagan could be the poster boy for our orphanage. His personality, smile, and laugh pleads with you not to feel sorry for us. Do not lament the past of the boys or their deplorable history and sorrowful testimony. Instead, live in the moment. Stay positive. Worship God with your heart mind and soul. Laugh often. It's the Reagan way.

"He will yet fill your mouth with laughter, and your lips with shouting." Job 8:21

Nicodemus's Watermelons; 10-10-13

If you've read the blog about what we grow, you realize that, on a large scale, we are limited to our crops. We have roughly fifteen acres of larger crop land. Vince, along with the boys, have cleared approximately a quarter of an acre about twenty feet west of our main building. This was rather difficult. The land has probably never been cultivated and was full of rocks. Every late afternoon for two weeks, the boys would gather there and clean up the patch of land for a small garden. This was laborious considering the fact that it took twenty-eight boys almost two weeks to get an adequate patch cleared. They planted okra, beans, and eggplant. Once planted, a portion of every evening is now spent weeding the garden and fighting off bugs.

While the boys were planting, each had a handful of watermelon seeds. Vince didn't think his seeds would grow, so he decided not to plant them and didn't want them to overrun the rest of the vegetables even if they could grow. Nicodemus begged Vince to let him plant the seeds. Vince finally relented and gave the seeds to Nicodemus. Nicodemus was pondering where to plant the seeds when he tripped and stumbled. The seeds went everywhere, towards the direction of the building. They were impossible to find. Everyone laughed and thought it was a lost cause…except Nicodemus. Every evening as the other boys would weed the garden, Nicodemus took a bottle of water and poured it on the area he thought the watermelon seeds landed. With the onset of the monsoon, Nicodemus forgot about the watermelons. Soon, though, the vines began to sprout.

When all was said and done, we harvested nine large watermelons because of Nicodemus's persistence. I joked around and named the corner of the area "Nicodemus's Patch." I love the sweet spirit of Nicodemus and his dedication to his watermelons. He definitely has a green thumb and I look forward to all of the delicious vegetables he grows in the near future. Is there anyone who would be interested in donating to help our vegetable garden?

Intentional Two-Fer; 10-17-13

People in the United States are crazy busy. I have found this even truer since traveling back from India. Confirming anyone to meet up with you or simply hang out is nearly impossible. People's schedules are too full. I know you agree, but this isn't a blog about how to cut out the excess fluff or even to bully you into guilt for not meeting up with me. Instead, it's a simple story about how I get around the "being too busy" part.

Let's face it, it is easier to get an elephant through the door of my bedroom than it is to cut most things out of my schedule. A few years back, I started doing some intentional two-for-one meetings with people. What I mean is that I tack a meet-up or hangout onto something I am already doing, or that the other person may already be doing. For example, when my buddy, Brandon Meekins, can't meet because he has to go grocery shopping for the family, I say, "Great! Let me come along." Simple right? Brandon gets to knock something off his honey-do list, and I get to spend quality time with him in the soup aisle. :) Kids need to be picked up from school and you will be in the carpool line indefinitely? Awesome! Pick me up first and let's make use of that time.

I have applied this concept to my life in India. I am pretty laid back in the United States, but I am always pedal-to-the-metal in India. I have twenty eight boys to look after and a huge building to keep up with, not to mention all the teams that filter through our home. Many times, I find myself too busy to spend quality time one-on-one with my boys, so I implemented the intentional two-fer. If I need to run an errand and the boys are around, I always take one of them with me on the motorcycle. It is great fun to be able to hang out with them even if it is just riding down the road to pick up eggs and water buffalo milk. I'm sure that listening to me babble the whole time gets annoying, but they are just happy to be with me, and they love the wind in their faces as we scream down the crazy Indian roads.

Our motorcycle recently broke down and we are trying to buy a new one. There is an American family that will be moving back to the United States soon and are willing to sell us their nice, new motorcycle. Please pray that God provides a way for us to purchase it. I don't want to miss the chance of spending quality time with my boys. I head back in December and I'm sure within a few hours of arrival, you will see me weaving in and out of goats on the road with one of my boys sitting in the front rolling his eyes at my latest cheesy story.

Untold Story of the Best Birthday Party Ever; 10-25-13

This is the full story of the now famous birthday party for the Shiloh Children's Home. It was a very typical Wednesday. I was sitting on a broken bunk bed that serves as a bench on our front porch. I had about twelve to fifteen boys all around me. Some were bouncing balls. Some were relaxing. A few were looking over my shoulder as I looked at photos on my phone. One boy, I don't remember who, asked me when my birthday was. I told him November 7 and asked him for his birth date. He had no clue. I then asked every boy and no one knew their birthday. I was dumbfounded. I, of course, have all of their records that have their birth dates and personal info on them, but it never occurred to me that they didn't know the actual dates. They were amused at my reaction. I pushed further and asked if they ever had a birthday party. The boys had no clue what I was talking about. In India, it is a custom for a person to give gifts on their own birthday. Many times, people from the community had visited our boys and passed out sweet treats in celebration of their birthday. Not only had none of the boys had their own birthday party, but they sat in amazement as I shared what birthday parties were and recalled some of my favorite childhood birthday party memories.

All in a moment, I looked at the boys and told them, "Guess what! Everyone's birthday is this coming Saturday and we are going to have a party!" The boys went crazy! They were so happy. Everyone gathered around and we planned out what kind of party they wanted to have. Since it is customary in India to give gifts on your birthday, I had each of them draw the name of another boy to give a gift. When each one had a name, I jotted down the gift they wanted to give. Some chose to give a ball. Some a kite. Others pencils and pens. We planned out the party to have cake and ice cream. For the rest of the week, the boys were so excited, but they had no idea what I had in store for them.

When Saturday came, the boys left for school and I headed into town to buy supplies, gifts, food, and decorations. I had it all organized and prepared for when they arrived at 1p.m. I wanted them to be center stage, so I allowed them to decorate it as they chose. We were lacking in decorations, so it was mainly decorated with Christmas lights and holiday-themed decorations. When they were done, it was time to begin.

I made them all sit on the floor. In India, it is customary for you to give a strand of garland to a person of respect that visits you. It is an honor to receive this garland of flowers. Think of it like a Hawaiian lei. It is full of roses and smells amazing. Every church and orphanage I have visited through the years has bestowed this flower garland on me. I wanted to convey to the boys that this was their day and the party was in their honor. I had them come, one by one, as we put the garland around their neck and also gave them a party hat.

Next, we had them come up to get a kite, then brought out the cake. No one had ever blown out candles, so I had an individual candle for each boy and they came up, one by one, to blow out their candle. They loved this!

Next, I surprised them by giving them the TV they had been asking about for over a year. It was candy apple red and awesome! After the TV, I acted like the party was over and walked away, however, I simply walked to my room and gathered the individual gift bags for them. In each bag were a new pair of shoes, a ball, pens and pencils, candy, and a few other items. They were so proud of the shoes that they refused to wear them for weeks. They were giddy, but I told them that the night was just getting started. Next, we cleared all the gifts and turned the sitting area into a dance floor. We danced like crazy for over an hour and had a blast. They took the flowers from the leis and threw them in the air over and over and over.

When the dancing was through, I introduced them to Bruce Lee. You've already read the blog post about Saturday nights with Bruce Lee. As they sat and enjoyed the movie, I had them come and get the snack tray I assembled for them. It had quite a few different items including namkeen, popcorn, and samosas.

After the movie time was over, we all slept like babies. Happy babies. The smile on their faces the next day was well worth it. It may not seem like much of a party, but I only spent about $10 on each boy and that included the TV. No big deal. Imagine being in the shoes of one of the boys! You have basically been abandoned by everyone close to you. Your day is filled with a schedule that has little to no variation. But for one day, you are treated like a king. The joy on their faces made it one of the top days of my life. It proved to the boys that they are valuable, their life is worth something, and that there are people who truly care and love them. I wouldn't trade that for anything in the world.

A shout out goes to all of the families and friends who recorded birthday videos for the boys or left sweet notes on my wall. A big thank you also goes out to Dr. Stephen Renfrow and all the others who also saw value in a birthday party and helped make it possible. Thank you so much. Just imagine how Christmas will be :)

Music and the Boys; 11-11-13

In January, I asked the boys what I could bring back for them when I returned for the summer. They were very timid. One boy said he wanted to eat chicken. Another said he wanted a rubber ball. When I asked them to be serious and ask for something bigger, Roman stood up and said he wanted "One LCD flat screen TV". HAHA. I asked them to be more reasonable. At this point the boys asked for instruments. They wanted a guitar and a keyboard. Through many prayers, God led us to create LOVOSO Music Initiative. LOVOSO stands for Love Orphans, Visit Orphans, Serve Orphans. Through donations, we were able to carry eight guitars, two keyboards, a mandolin, and a handful of harmonicas with us. We passed them out to four orphanages with over 1,000 orphans.

One Sunday, I decided to plunge them headfirst into music. I decided to just lay every instrument out and let them experiment with them. I didn't want to give them a lecture on how to treat the instruments or a bunch of rules. I just wanted them to fall in love. And they did!

At any given time of day, there is a boy strumming away on a guitar or poking at a keyboard. One of our keyboards has a song bank of 200 songs in it. The first song that comes up when you turn it on is the Disney song" A Whole New World". I heard it endlessly whenever the boys would turn on the keyboard. After hearing it about 200 times, I could not take it anymore. I heard the first ten notes of "A Whole New World" play and I had had enough. I ran around the corner to teach the boys how to use the song-bank so they could play a different song. To my amazement, there was one boy sitting at a keyboard but it wasn't the one with the song-bank. He was at a simpler keyboard that didn't even have a song-bank! The boy had taught himself to play "A Whole New World" by ear. I stood with my jaw open. His love of music was awesome. All of the children are like that. They love to sing at the top of their lungs and pound away on the simple instruments we have.

I have hired a young musician to come to the orphanage weekly and teach them basic guitar. Please pray for the boys as they learn the instruments and start writing their own songs.

Faith like a Child; 12-12-13

  I want to share with you something simple that happened this morning. As I was walking through the dining hall a few minutes ago back to the boys' room, Ricky was sitting at the table studying. Its 6 a.m., so I asked him if he was studying for an exam today. He said he was studying, but the exam wasn't until Monday. I told him that he was smart and that I believed he would do well. I then told him I would pray for him. In my mind, I didn't mean right that second, but as soon as I said it, Ricky took off his toboggan, knelt down on his knees, and waited for me to pray over him. That really got to me for many reasons. First is that he loves me enough to appreciate my prayers. Second, because it really made me think that if we are serious about something we take action. We do not wait until another time when we may forget. Third, how many times do I pray fully expecting that God will act? That is some serious faith right there.

  At that very second, he didn't want me to tell him I WOULD pray for him. He wanted me TO pray for him, right then. That very moment.

  If only I had the faith of Ricky!

Threshing Guar; 12-15-13

    As you may know, we have twenty acres of land here at
the orphanage. We have big dreams of what we want to do with the
land one day, but for now, it's all farmland. None of our boys have
much skill at farming (and I wouldn't want them to because it
would take away from their studies) so we have a few local
farmers that come in and do the work. We split the harvest with
them. Yesterday was threshing day for one of our crops. We
harvested guar and it needed to be threshed. Guar is Hindi for
"cow food". Many industries use it including the food industry that
relies on guar gum. The oil industry has even found a use for guar
in fracking. But for where we are, it's just cow food. Yesterday
after church was the time. The farmers brought over a tractor with
a threshing attachment and they went to work. I took some photos
of the process, but the farmers and their wives were much more

interested in my camera and actually seeing themselves. I hope to print these photos off for them soon.

New Desk; 12-20-13

It's not possible for me to go to the desk store. There is no Staples, or Target, or Walmart near me. Most of the times, if you need something like a desk or table, you have to really search. Where we are, you either have to build it yourself or have it built for you. When we inquired about getting a table fully built, it was way too expensive for our budget. We have thirty growing mouths to feed and the money is tight, so I came up with an idea.

We have old iron beds that the boys no longer use. I asked the builders if they could use our beds and just weld me a desk, and they did! It was ten times cheaper than having them make a new desk. The desk is awesome and it is just like our boys' desks. Instead of being thrown away and cast aside, we have rescued it and given it a new purpose. I prefer reclamation projects anyway :)

Good Things Come; 12-20-13

There's a saying that says good things come to those who wait. We do a lot of waiting here at the orphanage. We have all but stopped sharing our daily needs, but we are relying on God to meet those needs. We spend a lot of time in prayer letting God know what we think our needs are. And then we wait.

That is some nervous excitement right there. Knowing that God will provide, but wondering how exactly He will do it. I won't go into any details, but suffice it to say that we have been running low on resources and have had to be really creative this last week on making ends meet.

Enter in God's creative intervention. On three consecutive days, people from our community came by to lend a helping hand and provide for the children. On the first day, two young and hip couples showed up with a bunch of treats for the children to celebrate Christmas. They passed out gulab jamun, samosas, and Parle G biscuits to the boys. The next day, an officer in the army that was stationed close by came in to say that he was moving. He gave us two huge boxes of winter clothing for the boys. Finally, yesterday, an anonymous man came by and gave us enough money to buy chicken for the boys. As soon as he showed up, he was gone again. We didn't even catch his name. That makes it even better.

None of these gifts set the world on fire, but it provided exactly what we needed at that moment. It didn't leave us in abundance, but it was exactly what we needed. Just as God provided manna to the Israelites in their time of need, these gifts were our manna for that day.

Simply Having a Wonderful Christmastime; 12-31-13

So here is the official blog about Christmas. As some of you may have read on the Facebook page, I acquired a Santa Claus costume. I didn't even need to buy padding to go inside to recreate Nick's bowl full of jelly. :) Here in India, Santa Claus is named Christmas Father. I wanted to have the most fun possible without commercializing Christmas or taking away from the celebration of Christ. I decided to let their interaction with the Christmas Father to be one of fun and innocence, and not tied up in gift giving.

We had a bunch of gifts for them like balls and cricket bats, art supplies, toiletries, and various other knickknack toys along with their big presents- three different sized bikes for them all to enjoy and share. We set everything up on our main stage and had the boys locked in their two rooms. I dressed as Santa Claus and the fun began. They truly didn't expect to see Santa. Most had never seen him. The original lore of Saint Nicholas told of someone who came in the night and filled your shoes with fruit and candy, so I tried to keep it simple. I decided to give them each a Santa hat and a piece of candy from Santa. That way, they could have fun and not tie their memory to a gift.

I was a little worried that they would know it was me. I mean, how many 280 pound white dudes are walking around an obscure village in India? As I entered the room, it was apparent that most were just in awe. I disguised my voice and told them that their PAPA was at the train station picking up a guest. I even asked most of the boys what their name was to cover my tracks. I overheard one boy say, "That is not Papa, Papa knows my name." That made me beam from ear to ear. I do know his name :)

I passed out the hats and the candy and danced with each room as we sang Christmas carols. We locked them back in their rooms and I dashed off to my room to change back into my clothes. Within seconds I rushed back to their rooms and burst through the door screaming, "Where is he???? Where is Christmas Father??? I was at the train station and I rushed back as fast as I could!!!" The look on their faces at that moment was priceless. They proceeded to tell me how much fun they had singing and dancing with Christmas Father. They said he was fun but he didn't know any names. After their reenactments of what I was already a part of, I made them all line up at the door ready to go out and see their presents just like me and all my cousins used to do at my Grandmother's house for many years. My cousins and I would line up in front of Grandmother's bathroom, making sure we didn't step on the metal grate that covered up the furnace in the floor. We wanted so badly to stand closer to the door to the living room but knew that the furnace cover would give us a burning we would never forget. I remembered this as I made the boys line up. The boys had no idea what was waiting for them. Not a single boy has ever owned a bike and only about seven of them have ever even been on a bike. When they walked out to see what was there, you would have thought each one of them had won the lottery. They barely looked at their individual prizes at first. They were all line up to ride the bikes. There was a small bike, a medium bike, and a large bike. We mostly have small to medium boys so that line was super long. Vikas is one of our small boys, but he couldn't wait. He jumped on the biggest bike and took it around. The funny thing is that his feet didn't even reach the pedals, so he pedaled with one foot and kept going around and around and around. What a sight! The pictures and video tell it better than I can.

This was the night of December 23. On the 24th, we had a Christmas service here on our campus and around 1,000 people from all over our area came out. I was only able to speak for ten minutes before JP and I had to catch a train to Kota.

The train ride seemed to take forever and we finally reached Kota at 2 a.m. The next morning, we awoke early to enjoy Christmas day celebrations with 600 orphans at our sister home and another 1,000 people from the community. I didn't like being away from the boys, but I had to speak and I had a really good time. After the service, the ministry did something really fun and helpful. They designated fifty families from the community to give Christmas gifts to those who had a need. They passed out cookware, sewing machines, and bicycles. The neat thing was that the ministry asked local businessmen and guests to stand up and donate the items. One by one, the guests went on stage and gave money for the gifts and personally donated items to the families as they came up. I didn't want to be left out of the fun, so I donated two sewing machines in Susan's honor to two older ladies that had a need.

What a wonderful Christmas time it was! I got to celebrate with the boys, sing festive songs, dress up as Santa, speak about Jesus, and give gifts to those in need. Thank you so much for all of you that pray for us. We truly live day to day and are only able to make it by the grace of God. He gets the glory for everything that is given. Thank you so much for remembering us in prayer. Now on to the New Year!

We are grateful to the ones who donated these things, but more importantly we give thanks to God because we know He heard our cries and He answered us... with manna.

All Creatures Great and Small; 1/5/14

I am so happy right now I can hardly contain it! We are in a slow process here at the orphanage to become fully sustainable. We have twenty acres of land that we are working hard to cultivate with diverse crops. We also want to have as many animals as we possibly can to produce milk, meat, and eggs. The Agape Sunday School Class from the Baptist Church of Beaufort, South Carolina gave a very generous gift to the orphanage. With their gift, we are in the process of buying a bunch of animals. We have spent the last week building a buffalo hut and chicken coops. And within the last hour, I bought two water buffalo!!!!! I bought a mother and a baby!!!!! Both are female. The mother is currently giving two gallons of milk a day and should increase to three gallons with a better diet and warmer weather. I am so stinking excited!! We plan to buy two goats, fifty chickens and fifty rabbits within this week.

I need you to pray specifically for something. Although both of our buffaloes are healthy, there has been a major disease going around and within the last month, 75% of the water buffaloes in our area have died. I am trusting that God will not allow our buffaloes to die. The boys really need the milk and I beg you to pray for the health of our animals. SO excited!

Thank you soooo much, Agape Class!!!!!

Happy Birthday, Ronnie! 1-11-14

Tomorrow is Ronnie's tenth birthday. Today, I took him to hang out, eat, and do a little gift buying. First, we stopped off at the market to buy the food rations for the orphanage for the rest of the month. Then, we stopped by a shop and bought him a jacket and some cricket equipment.

We went out to my favorite little fast food joint in the city called The Grill. Up to that point, Ronnie was a bundle of excitement, but as soon as we walked in, you'd have thought someone killed his dog. He went pale and looked terrified. Not thinking too much of it, we ordered almost one of everything on the menu. We ordered a pizza, a veg burger for him, paneer tikka bread, french fries, and smiley face potatoes. When we were seated, I asked him how many times he had been to a restaurant. His answer was "never." No wonder my little feller was so pale. He was scared to death! He had no idea how to act or what to do. I ordered him a Pepsi and he chugged it all within twenty seconds. He started to warm up a little and by the time the food came, he was so relaxed that he ate the whole burger, half of the pizza, all my fries, two pieces of paneer bread, and three smiley faces. And he drank another Pepsi! I was so worried he was going to lose his lunch on the motorcycle ride back. But it got me to thinking, how many times have I eaten at a restaurant in the last ten years. Fast food included? How many times have you?? What was just a normal thing for me was something this sweet boy had NEVER experienced. Man, the little things sometimes can be so powerful.

Thank God today for the little things you take for granted.

Nemo HAD A BIRTHDAY????? 1/14/14

    I thought I knew everything about the boys. Man was I wrong. I had poured over their biographies and their folders and memorized some pretty random stuff. But I didn't know everything. I told someone here that I was creating a database of the boys' stats including name, age, date of birth, the date they arrived here, and school grade. He informed me that he already had a list. When I compared his list with all my info, one thing stood out....

    Nemo had different dates of birth on the different forms. One said May 6; the other said January 6. So, I went straight to Nemo and asked him. He said January 6. Nothing worse than finding out on January 12 that you have missed a kid's birthday! Man, did I feel bad! To be honest, I don't think Nemo cared. He had never celebrated his birthday, and I don't think he even realized it had passed. But I'm sure he was jealous of Ronnie's party.

    There is no time like the present, so yesterday we celebrated Nemo's seventh birthday. I tried to make it extra special. I have stumbled across a method that I think I will implement for all the boys. I took Nemo out with me on the motorcycle, which may have been his personal highlight. We then took him to buy clothes and a toy. On our way back, we stopped off for a meal of his choice, just the two of us. When we returned home, we had a cake and sang him "Happy Birthday". As soon as I started cutting the cake, the power went out. Go figure. It is customary for the birthday boy or girl to cut the cake and feed it to a loved one. He cut the cake and gently fed me. I proceeded to cut a little piece with loads of icing and smashed it in his face. Good times.

It is amazing to me how normal these boys are after having been deprived of affection. When I first got here, they were sweet but standoffish. I am a huge hugger. I cannot pass a single one of them without hugging their necks and telling them that I love them. The Hindi phrase for " I Love You" is "May Pyar Karta Hoon." This is how it sounds, not necessarily how it is written. I repeat that phrase about two to three hundred times a day, and that is no exaggeration. There is no time like the present, and i am trying to make up for lost time. Slowly, they are warming up to the affection, and now a few of them hug me before I can reciprocate.

Nemo was no different. He loved being the center of attention. In a country of a billion people, it is hard to have an individual identity. It is hard to constantly show the boys that each and every one of them is special to me. I now know each and every one of their laughs, their strides, and their whistles! I can pick out each boy walking in the dark even when the power is out. To me, they are not just one in a billion. They are my sons and I love them each more than I can ever imagine.

Thank you, Nemo, for being the sweet, little, quiet boy with a tender smile. May you have the best year yet!

God Ain't Forgot Us Yet; 1/14/14

If you haven't noticed already, we don't make it a habit of asking for money. We do have something called Project 450 that supports the boys, but fundraising is not our first focus. It is our belief that God is in control and He is the one providing for our every need. In turn, we give Him the glory for everything, not our brilliant social media or marketing campaigns. This, of course, doesn't mean that we don't have needs. Boy, do we ever! Our response is to encourage people to ask God how **they** should be involved instead of us telling them how they should be involved. This takes a lot more faith, but it is also humbling seeing exactly how God provides.

A couple of days ago we had a need, so I specifically prayed for it. Susan called me later that night and said someone anonymously sent $25 in cash to our P.O. BOX in the United States. No name. No return address. That amount was almost to the penny of what I had prayed for. Thank you, Mr. or Mrs. Anonymous, and thanks be to God for hearing my ever simple prayer.

Today is January 14. It is a holiday all over India sometimes known as Kite Day. It is one of the major festivals in the state of Rajasthan, known as "Makar Sankranti" or "Sankrant" in the Rajasthani language. This day is celebrated with some special Rajasthani delicacies and sweets like Pheeni (either with sweet milk or sugar syrup dipped),Til-paati, Gajak, kheer, Pakodis, Puwas, Til-ladoos, etc. "

God knew that our supplies were running low because five different groups of people have come by and dropped off food for the children. Five groups of people!!! Man, what a blessing! It started out this morning with a family bringing a full breakfast for the children. Then, someone brought a bunch of pantry items like flour, sugar, salt, and other spices. Another came by and brought A LOT of bananas. No sooner had they left, a man on a motorcycle stopped and gave the children sweet treats, peanuts, and sesame seed treats. He gave them each a pencil case with school supplies, and as he was still passing out the treats, ANOTHER guy showed up to give the children salty snacks and sweet treats. It all happened this morning in a short amount of time. It would not surprise me if a few other people showed up between now and bedtime. What a joy it is to know that not only is God providing for us, but we also get to spend some time with our community that truly has a heart for the well being of these boys.

God hasn't forgotten us. Our needs are great, even overwhelming most of the time, and our reliance on Him has never been greater. Seeing the way He provides gives me a greater peace than I could ever create for myself or the boys.

We will keep praying and God will keep providing. Join us in this prayer.

Prayer Room; 1/15/14

We have about twenty eight rooms in our orphanage, give or take a closet or two. One of my first objectives was to re-work every room and plan what we should do for each. When I arrived here, most of the rooms stored junk. I got rid of most of it and consolidated the rest. With the remaining empty rooms, I made four guest rooms and set aside one for an office. I allotted one for a study hall for the boys and one for a computer lab. We have a storeroom to keep our newly laid chicken eggs as well as their feed. In the future, there will be a music room and a sport equipment room.

By far, my favorite room, and my top priority, was the prayer room. After months of trying to obtain the necessary items, we finished it as of yesterday, The room is not very big but is enough for us to fit and be cozy. I have placed twelve dry erase boards on the wall so we can record all of our prayer requests, and yours too. For our 6pm prayer time, we come into the room and sing for about ten minutes. Then, we go one by one through the prayer requests on the boards. We have boards for requests from the United States, for Indian requests, and one specifically for the boys' personal requests. Almost every boy is praying either for the salvation of his family members or the protection of his family from persecution. That is literally their own prayer requests. When I was that age, I probably prayed for a bike or a girl to like me. These boys are praying that their families will come to know the one true God. Heart-wrenching and humbling. We also have a couple of boards of praises for when God answers our prayers.

After we pray, we sing and we are done. One thing to note - I have encouraged the boys whenever they walk by the prayer room to stop in and quickly go down the list. For the last two days, I have observed boy after boy wander in for five or ten minutes and pray on their own. How's your prayer life? I know mine could use some dedication like that.

I fully believe that God hears children's prayers faster than adults who have too much junk in the way. I mean, look at this verse, "See that you do not look down on one of these little ones. For I tell you that their angels in heaven always see the face of my Father in heaven." - Matthew 18:10" It says right there that their angels are hanging out with God himself, 24/7! So, if you have a prayer request, send it our way. I have twenty eight prayer warriors ready to intercede on your behalf.

It is amazing what God is doing at our humble orphanage. The boys are growing, learning, and constantly on the move. They rise early and pray. The go to school all day, six days a week. They play hard and have more chores than I had at their age (it is a big facility). **They worship like it's their job**. And they love, love, love. They love their families, and each other, and me.

Please don't let how awesome our boys are deceive you into stopping your prayers for them. We need your prayers now more than ever. We are surrounded by people who are far from like-minded. We are in a constant daily struggle to provide. Yet God miraculously provides. Every. Single. Day. Please don't stop praying. We need it!

Our boys are diligent in their prayer life. Our prayer room is filled with prayer requests that the boys go through individually and with passion. They reach their hands out to the names on our prayer wall, begging God to heal many from cancer, disease, and other sicknesses. They ask God to provide traveling mercies for those who are on journeys, and they pray for God to provide comfort and peace for grieving families. The boys pray this for you.

So, I once again beg you to remember our boys in prayer. Pray for their daily needs. Pray for their education. Pray for their future. Pray that God will use them mightily. If you have a specific prayer request, please let me know. The boys will intercede with passion for you. I pray you will do the same for them.

Day to Day; 1/15/14

Many people have asked me what a typical day looks like here at the orphanage. In fact, occasionally my own wife asks, "What exactly DID you do today?" Even though every day varies, here is just a glimpse:

5:30   Staff wakes up and begin cooking breakfast for children

5:45   Boys wake up and pray

6:45   Boys prepare for school

7:15   Boys eat breakfast

7:45   Boys head out to school

8:30-9 Staff prayer

9-12   I personally spend time working the land and animals and other labor projects around the building including the laundry. I do on average 30 loads of laundry a week. SERIOUSLY.

12-3   I travel into the city to buy supplies. With 20,000 square feet and 35 people living here, there are always things to buy.

3pm   Boys arrive from school and begin homework

4pm   Boys begin their work and chores and have canteen

5pm   Boys play cricket and marbles and whatever else they want

6pm   We have one hour of prayer time

7pm   Boys eat dinner

8pm   Boys continue their homework

9pm   Boys go to bed and my day begins.

When I say my day begins, I mean according to American time. This is when I write these blogs (which is right now.) I spend time assisting teams and people who will be coming to visit us. I get the honor of interacting with our donors who make this whole thing happen. I also get the chance to unwind and read.

Around midnight, I emerge from my office and lock everything up and head to bed. I am a person that thrives on eight hours of sleep. I can function with little sleep, only by the grace of God, even though I am always the first one up and the last one down. I haven't had eight hours of sleep, or anything close to it, since coming to Shiloh. My Fitbit says I average about two hours and thirty minutes of sleep a night

Please be praying for us as we go through our day to day.

Whatever Happened to "The Sound of Music?"; 1/15/14

Everyone has seen "The Sound of Music". If not, shame on you. It is the brilliant classic movie starring Julie Andrews as a nun who comes to live with a family and teaches them to sing, dance, and play music. Their rigid world comes to life when she enters. Surely you know the line, "The hills are alive with the sound of music." The movie has some tense points but still teems with wholesome goodness. I mean, how great is it when they escape over the Alps into Switzerland as the mean Nazis have car trouble?

Well, many people think I am living the real life "Sound of Music". Although some days are near perfect, some are comical and gut-wrenching. Take today, for instance. We have a small team coming to rewire our orphanage next week. I have spent weeks getting their guest rooms ready, and yesterday I bought new space heaters for them. I wanted to check them out to make sure they were working properly since sometimes it's hit or miss here getting electronics to work properly. So, I decided to use one in my room last night. I plugged it in my surge protector and it worked fine. All. Night. Long. Until 5:45 am when it proceeded to set my wall on fire. Yeah. Really. That happened. I didn't smell anything or hear anything, but I woke up and saw the whole wall socket ablaze and melting. It quickly ran down the whole cord. As quick as a flash, I jumped up and yanked it out of the wall. It was a jerk reaction, but what a stupid move. Although it didn't harm me at all, it easily could have jolted the literal poop out of me. What a way to start the day!

Soon after the boys left for school, I was walking around the land and saw wrapper after wrapper of candy. I also saw lots of trash everywhere. Keep in mind that our boys had so many candies and snacks yesterday. Even though I always encourage them not to litter, those pleadings apparently went unheeded. I spent three hours picking up trash this morning and barely made a dent. Bear in mind, we have twenty acres.

I wasn't whistling Dixie this morning, that's for sure. And I sure as heck wasn't singing, "These Are a Few of my Favorite Things." It was more like "These are the boys that I want to strangle." Of course, that's a joke, but haven't we all had times where people just infuriate us when they just don't get it? Instead of beating them down and making them feel horrible, I came up with a better plan.

I decided to split all the boys up into eight work crews. Two crews would clean their rooms. Two crews would clean our sanctuary and common areas. One crew would clean the kitchen and dining hall, another crew would be responsible for picking up trash outside, another crew would tend our new garden, and the last crew would look after our animals. Each team is made up of age appropriate boys who can do each particular job. I also assigned a team leader to be in charge of the task. Our goal is to do these tasks for thirty minutes-one hour every day after they get home from school. What started as the boys being upset turned into a golden opportunity to share with them the goal of personal responsibility (which was also my sermon subject this past Sunday.) It also provides a tangible avenue for instilling leadership in the boys.

Although we are not the Von Trapp family, I wouldn't trade these boys for anything in the world, even if we have to "Climb Ev'ry Mountain."

What's in a Name? 3/14/14

I love naming things. I named my first truck Molly after my kindergarten crush. I love giving nicknames to friends like my college friend, Benjamin, or as I called him, Ben Jammin. I love naming regular old stuff...mostly, I name stuff Elvis. He was my first music love, ya know? I named my dog Elvis, my guitar Elvis, and my first laptop was Elvis, ad nauseum. I have had fun naming festivals that I started...Anyone remember the Peacemaker Festivals? I had a record company called PeaceFreek. I ran an organization called Tyro Mavin Worldwide. Currently, we have a jewelry company called Chunky Junk, a music initiative called LOVOSO, and our non-profit to orphans, of course is No Longer Orphans.

I love the process of naming things... the research phase, picking out possibilities, and the reaction from people when you give them possible options. Even the naming of this book was somewhat of a competition from longtime supporters of No Longer Orphans. It is no secret at the orphanage that we are expanding and will have various initiatives which enable us to become sustainable. I would like to introduce you to each of those initiatives, their names, and how I set about naming them.

First off, as you may know, the actual name of the children's home is Shiloh. One of my top three artists of the last twenty years is Andrew Peterson. On his first album, he has a song entitled "Shiloh". This was the name of his childhood home. The song calls to you as you listen, "Get on home to Shiloh." I thought it a fitting tribute to thank Andrew by naming the orphanage Shiloh. As I did a little research, the name became a better fit than I had first thought. In the Old Testament, there was a city named Shiloh. As one historian noted, Shiloh was known as a "place of rest for weary travelers". Wow, what better moniker could we possibly find? We truly want to be a place where weary travelers and friends alike can come and rest their weary bones while helping us transform the lives of these amazing boys. Thanks so much, Andrew Peterson, for being a part of my life these last few years through your music. Our boys absolutely adore every album you have done. I would highly recommend that everyone "discover" Andrew Peterson, if you have not done so already, and buy all of his albums.

The second initiative we are building is the auto initiative. Although it is affectionately known as the Auto Initiative here, once we have our fleet of cars, we will need to call it something in India. We have settled on Sound Travels. This is a play on word in three ways. First of all, sound truly does travel. Second, "sound" also means stable, competent, and reliable. The third way is because of what the initiative is named after. Another one of my influential artists that has impacted my life is Jon Foreman of Switchfoot. He brilliantly wrote a song called "The Sound". My favorite line from the song is, "There is no song louder than love."

What we are trying to do with the auto initiative is to share the love and care for our boys in creative ways. The "sound" of our love should be more than just spoken words. It should be in our every action and thought. Thus the naming of the Auto Initiative is Sound Travels. The Auto Initiative is meant to be a way for us to impact our local community and sustainably provide for ourselves by having a fleet of auto rickshaws and small cars that we rent out to people who would otherwise have no transportation.

Finally we come to our animals and farm. We have a fast-growing herd of animals that currently number two water buffalo, three rabbits, eight dogs, and twenty-five chickens. The goats and other barnyard favorites will quickly follow. We may even have a camel in the coming year. We also have twenty acres of farmland where we grow a bunch of crops like wheat, guar, mustard, dal, and corn. I thought about the naming of this farm more than the others because it's the closest to my heart. I have settled on naming it "Resplendent Farms". The word resplendent means "to shine brilliantly, be radiant, dazzling, gleaming." This epitomizes the life I want for my boys. I want them to be the shining glory of our Risen Lord. Resplendent is a tribute to my favorite author, artist, singer, songwriter, poet of all time... Bill Mallonee. Bill was the stalwart behind the Vigilantes of Love. They recorded one of my favorite songs of all time, "Resplendent". The song is about triumph through heartache, joy from pain. It reminds me of the dustbowl generation who literally had nothing but somehow, many of them, through gritted teeth, chose joy. My own grandfather lost his first wife and firstborn to disease. This, is similar to the story of my boys. Even though the world has discarded them and expects them to fail, they are resplendent. I implore you to listen to the song and rejoice with me that we are all resplendent despite our shortcomings. Thank you so much Mr. Bill for your lyrics that have been a main guiding rod in my life. Please check out his stuff at http://billmalloneemusic.bandcamp.com/merch. Blessings to you if you fall in love with his music as much as I haveHe has produced over sixty albums over the last twenty years. He doesn't know this, but I named my new motorcycle Mallonee.

So there you have it - the new names and the reasons behind them. I introduce to you:

Shiloh Children's Home
Sound Travels
Resplendent Farms

Girl Scout Cookie Check; 4/10/14

There are many creative ways that people have helped out our boys and our Shiloh Home. People have sent donations, sent cool things in the mail, etc. One of the boys favorite groups is the Wake Forest Girl Scout Troop 602. They gathered Christmas gifts that we were able to give our boys on Christmas day. They actually sent over Valentines cards for every boy along with two boxes of Girl Scout cookies that the boys LOVED.

My favorite thing so far was that they decided to collect all of their proceeds from the sale of cookies and donated it to the boys. My friend, Victoria, is the troop leader. I joked with Victoria that if she insisted on doing a big ceremony and presentation, then I demanded an oversized check. You know, like lhe ones at golf or tennis tournaments. The HUGE ones. I told her I wasn't showing up unless she could do that. I was really kidding, but as I showed up tonight at Joyner Park in Wake Forest to talk to the girls, they presented me with the check! It was awesome! I took photos of me with the girls holding the check. I couldn't let a big check go to waste. I have always wanted to have one, so I got a few crazy shots of me enjoying my check. You can check out the photo on our blog at http://www.nolongerorphans.org/girl_scout_cookie_check and see photos of me doing some crazy athletic poses with the check.

59

SEND MONEY! (Published on 04/11/14)

I was reminded this morning of the funny lyrics of a Newsboys song. They are:

"Mom & Dad,

I'm fine. How are you?

I have joined a

Small circus (that much is true). I'm a

Little malnourished, but try to relax.

Could you find a better photo for the milk carton backs?

Send money."

It's a funny, catchy song.

Anyway, my best friend and coworker, JP, sent me two photos of the boys this morning. In both photos, the boys are holding up a sign that says, "Papa, Do not worry." JP told me that he accidentally took the first photo without giving warning, so it just came across as super funny to me. It's almost as if the boys are imprisoned in a horrible jail on a lonely island with horrible captors, but snuck out a photo letting me know that everything is ok. I kept looking at the photo for Morse code to see if anyone was blinking that things are not as they seem. HAHA! The expression on their faces just screams "HELP, SEND MONEY!" It was only after I pointed out their blank looks did JP send a second photo. I had a good laugh to say the least.

All jokes aside, it was so sweet to get these pictures this morning of my precious boys telling me not to worry about them. You really should meet them one day. Your life will be better for getting to know these boys a little more.

Birthdays are Special; 4/16/14

Do you remember details of a particular birthday party? I am sure most of us do. No one remembers their first birthday, but I am sure a lot of others stand out. For me, two birthdays rise above the rest.

The first was my thirteenth birthday. We were rather poor at the time and the presents were scarce. That is not my favorite thing, although I do remember getting one gift. The game was on the original Nintendo and was called.....Sky Shark. It was one of the best gifts ever! I played it for hours on end. I have included a video of the game that retrospectively looks pretty bland and bad, but at the time, the game was awesome. My favorite memory of that day, though, was just being with my family. We went out to eat at a 50's themed diner in Valdosta, Georgia before going to see the theatrical classic, "Look Who's Talking". The time spent with my family was a memory I will never forget.

The other birthday I remember like it was yesterday was my sixteenth. I had been saving up for months to buy a truck. I gave all the money I had saved to my dad and told him to surprise me…and he did. He took the money and bought a 1980 Chevy Scottsdale long bed truck. He painted it midnight black and put a pretty decent stereo system in it. I stayed in that truck overnight just sitting there listening to my favorite cds. I still remember the way it smelled…like new paint and old vinyl seats. It smelled like it was MINE! I will never forget that day or the gift of the "Black Stallion".

For our boys at Shiloh, birthdays were never a big thing. In fact, none of the boys ever had a party and most didn't even know their birthdate. Well, not until August 10, 2013. That was the day we had a celebration birthday party like never before. Every boy was celebrated.

We will continue to do that. I am really working hard on helping the boys realize their individuality. That is hard in a country of one billion people. However, helping each boy realize their value to me, and more importantly to God, is crucial.

We celebrate every boy's birthday like they are the King of the Castle. My little routine is to take them with me around 6 pm on their birthday. We drive around for a few minutes on the motorcycle and head to a shop to buy them a new change of clothes. They love trying on the new jeans and shirt, and they love wearing them home. I also buy them something fun and impractical like a cricket bat, toy car, or soccer ball. Then, we go out to eat at the only fast food joint in our city. It is vegetarian and choices are a little different, but we have a blast. We eat pizza, fries, veggie burgers, and drink Pepsi. I remember Ronnie's day. He is normally boisterous, inquisitive, and full of nervous energy. As we sat and ate our fries, he was quiet and his face was stone cold. I asked him what his favorite restaurant was and he stared back blankly. I asked him how many times he had eaten out and he looked around the room and then said "just now." He had never been out to eat before. He wasn't scared; he was soaking it all in. When we got back to the orphanage, I could hear him telling every boy of the awesome adventure he had. You see, his birthday was the first one we celebrated this year. On our way back to the home, we stopped and bought a cake for us all to enjoy, complete with his name on it.

As we sang "Happy Birthday" to him, he truly got tears in his eyes as he looked at me. I knew how special he felt. This has been told to me verbally by every boy now in their own way. One of our boys, Peter, is normally super quiet. He is active, but isn't verbal. He just soaks it all in. After he and I ate for his birthday, we rode around for a few minutes before heading home. As we hit an open section of highway, I gunned my motorcycle just a bit and yelled, "wooooooo." At that moment, Peter reached his arms around me, gave me a huge bear hug, and said, "Papa, I love this. I am so happy."

These are some of the things I think we take for granted in life. I am not suggesting that you take your birthdays for granted, but I think we assume that everyone, everywhere has the chance to be royalty for a day like we do. That's all I want for my boys - just a day they can know that I supremely love them for who they are as an individual, that they matter, and that their life has purpose.

As we close out each boy's birthday, there is a time of simple ceremony. We light their cake, we sing "Happy Birthday" to them in a crazy Indian key, and they blow out their candles. In India, it is a custom for each person on their birthday to give gifts to others. For every boy, I give them a huge bag of candy for them to share with their classmates and teacher. Why should they not have that joy simply because they live at an orphanage? Another tradition is for the birthday boy to cut his own cake and pass out a piece to every person in attendance. Our boys do this, but before they do, they always feed me the very first piece. I cry every time. What a sign of humility to give your first piece away to your father. Shortly after they feed me, I take a piece and playfully shove it in their face, in their ears, or down their chest. What is a good birthday cake worth if it can't be smeared on your loved one?

The boys' birthdays are glorious days. It is a day for each of them to give simple gifts to their peers and elders. It is a day for me to celebrate their life with some time of fellowship and laughter, and it is a time for all of us to gather in prayer for the life of that boy and pray that he will be blessed in his coming year. I pray that one day, when he is my age, he will look back on his birthdays, just like I do, with fondness and memories he will never forget.

Hot, Hot Heat; 4/21/14

In case you didn't know, it gets HOT in India. I mean REALLY hot. Our city's highest recorded temperatures was 125 degrees!. Here I am this morning, a little bit on the cold side. It is currently forty-seven degrees as I look out my window. Meanwhile, this week at the orphanage it will be no less than 100 degrees during the days, with every day topping out around 108 or 109, and it's not even the worst yet. It will be in the high teens within the next three weeks. I mean 118 degrees kind of heat. It is true that our summer season in India is a little ahead of the United States, and the hottest month is May. It is also true that our area is a bit more of a "dry heat." It reminds me of the comedian who joked about dry heat. He said "....dry heat. A bonfire is also dry, but you don't see me sticking my butt in it." We have a fully functioning farm. If it was too dry, we wouldn't be able to grow a thing. So, please remember our boys as the temperatures creep in the mid 80s in the United States and the common motto becomes,"its soooo hot."

This is not meant as a public service announcement. Our boys seem to manage very well. As we in the United States tolerate certain amounts of heat before we scurry back to cars with air conditioning, as we walk out of buildings with air conditioning, our boys main way of cooling down is to lay under a ceiling fan and press their face against the cool marble floor. And there's nothing wrong with that.

Say a little pray for the ones around the world who have nowhere to hide. Be grateful that someone invented air conditioning (I know I am!), and remember when ninety degrees seems SOOO hot, somewhere in India there is a little boy with his face against a marble floor, cooling down from a long cricket game, thinking to himself, "120 degrees ain't that bad." :)

Be blessed no matter where you are.

Sustainability and a goat named Mrs Eatin'; 5/5/14

God moves in mysterious ways, His wonders to perform. If you have read our website's funding page, you will soon realize how we operate and raise funds. For the most part, we do not share every need we have. We do this partly because of over-saturation. We do not want to be an organization that constantly inundates you with plea after plea. No one likes that. Also, we do not share some of our immediate needs because we first take them to God. If He leads us to keep things quiet, we do.

We would like to share some needs with you at this time based on the individual need, the pressing of God, and because of the encouragement of a few close friends of No Longer Orphans. But first, a sad but cool story that just happened.

Last week, I received a frantic call from JP that our water buffalos, Lady and Agape, were missing. We had no idea what happened to them. Our first thought was that they were stolen, but it seems that after some time and investigation, the gate was inadvertently left open and a couple of boys forgot to tie up the animals. Open gate=missing buffalos. We haven't found them and will likely never find them. Grace applied to the boys who made the mistake, and new rules about open gates.

However, we are still saddened about the loss of our beloved buffalos. A church Sunday school donated the funds to purchase them and we really needed the animals. They provided milk for us every day and we used the extra milk to sell and get funding for other food.

When I got the call from JP, I was in Tennessee visiting a bunch of families who have a heart for India and want to establish schools and orphanages. I shared the story with them. Many of the families have adopted from India. The following day, one of the girls who was adopted from India had her first birthday party. She turned five and had a wonderful party. In lieu of gifts, the family requested donations for our orphanage, and by the grace of God, $600 was given which is exactly what we need to purchase a new buffalo.

The incident made us realize a few things. First, we want to be as close to fully sustainable as we can be which means having multiple animals that we can milk or get eggs from. The loss of the buffalo hit us hard. We lost good income and the boys are without their daily milk. Now, we are adding a section on the donate page for you to help us purchase a water buffalo. We need at least five water buffalos to help us towards sustainability.

Another really cool thing happened while we were in Tennessee. We stayed with Tim and Liz Eaton who are both teachers. Liz shared all about our orphanage with her 6th grade class. The children wanted to take up an offering. Liz legally cannot have anything to do with it or encourage it, but the kids on their own took up an offering and gave it to Tim without Liz's knowledge or consent. The kids took up $122 which we are going to use to purchase a goat. Goats are around $100 in our area. We have decided to call the goat Mrs. Eatin', named after Liz and the fact that goats eat everything. We will post pics of Mrs. Eatin' and the buffalo as soon as we purchase them.

All that to say, we have added animals back to our donate page. If you feel led to help us purchase an animal, we will let you name it and also send a certificate signed by all of the boys in appreciation for partnering with us. The links to the animals are below. Who doesn't want to name a goat after their ex-girlfriend, angry boss, or your best friend?

Thoughts on Mother's Day; 5/12/14

     Mother's Day is always a flood of emotions for me. I have the greatest mother in the world. She is selfless, compassionate, God-honoring, loyal, and determined. She has had over twenty surgeries since I was a boy and continues to deal with debilitating incurable injuries on a daily basis. She has had three surgeries in the last six months and is nowhere near the finish line of recovery. However, I cannot remember a time when she complained or blamed God. I want to be like that. A blessed Happy Mother's Day to my mother.

     I am also overwhelmed at this time for many reasons. First, I weep for my wife because we are unable to have children. I know this is a huge desire for her and she continues to plead to God for a baby. If God can give Abraham and Sarah a child, He can do the same for us. I am also brokenhearted this time of year because of immense losses to those around me. We have two different families from our home church that lost their newborn babies on the day they were born. I cannot imagine or fathom their loss. My heart weeps for them. Also, one of my friends from church lost his mother unexpectedly just days before Mother's Day. My heart mourns with him.

My father's mother passed away on Mother's day in 1962. My father was eight years old. I have seen the way this has shaped my father's life and I can't help but shed a tear when I think of the an eight-year-old boy visiting his mother in the hospital with a Mother's Day card and hearing the news. There are truly no words.

I also think about being entrusted with the lives of twenty-eight boys. Each is under our care because every person in their life has abandoned them. The daily stuff they have to deal with blows me away. It is a responsibility we do not take lightly. As mentioned above, we can't have biological children, so these twenty-eight boys are ours. The love we have for these boys cannot be put into words. It's a redemption story. Our boys fill the void in our hearts and help heal our wounds. We have boys who have no mothers. We have boys whose mother is handicapped and invalid. We have boys whose mothers want nothing to do with them. And now, we have Susan who is a mother to them all.

On this day, I am mourning the loss of babies over the past two weeks, the loss of a friend's mother, the remembrance of my father's mother, and the pain of not having our own babies. However, I am thankful for the sweetest mother in the world, and I am thankful for a sweet wife who chooses to be the mother for twenty-eight boys.

My heart aches, but it is also full of God's goodness and mercy. Remember our boys this week as they think of their mothers. My father once said, "A boy will always remember his mother's face." That's the way it should be.

It Takes a Village; 5/13/14

As some of you may know, we have been back and forth the last year caring for the orphans. We were mostly in India, but it has been a year of transitions as we move over for good. That time is here and we make the move next week. This next week will be especially hectic, so I wanted to share this with you now.

You have heard the saying that it takes a village to raise a child. This is true. For us, our village is worldwide. We cannot do it without the larger community assisting us with prayers and donations. This is especially true this week and I want to share this with you specifically.

Last week, I put up a post about how you can donate animals to our orphanage and name them in honor of whatever you want. A few did just that and I want to share their stories.

First off, the Brocato family has decided to donate a goat. The mother, Nicole, says her kids thought she was crazy when she told them. Well, they will believe it soon enough when the goat is purchased and they can see it for themselves. They are working on a name and I will let you know as soon as they come up with something.

Crystal Perdue has donated five chickens and two pillow and sheet sets for the boys. Thank you so much, Crystal. Fresh eggs are the bee's knees!

Amanda Raines from Welcome Baptist Church in Greenville, South Carolina donated money for a goat. We have decided to name the goat "Manna" because God has provided. Amanda was telling me that her mother wrote a book entitled "Gathering Manna" in telling of the miraculous ways that God has provided for her family. What a great honor to name a goat in remembrance that God is faithful. You can learn more of the full story and the book at their website -

http://www.gatheringmanna.org/

Finally, Susan and I were selling jewelry at a festival the other day to raise funds for the orphans. We were sharing space, selling Chunky Junk jewelry, and working next to a nice couple who manned the Red Cross booth about the children. What a great day it was just talking and enjoying new friends! When we got home, we discovered they had donated money for a goat in remembrance of our brief time together. The goat will be named Wallace since that is the city where the festival was held. Thank you so much Gerri and Dean Hanson for the gift of Wallace.

See how easy it is to have an impact on our children??? For the time being, I am going to remove the goat donation button because three is exactly what we need for now. I will probably add it back at the end of the summer. In the meantime, remember that we still need at least two more water buffaloes and dozens more chickens. Chickens are only $10 for two hens. Please help if you can. I will update this once I get situated and buy the five chickens and three goats

6/12/2014

For all those in the triangle without power, I feel your pain. Our power goes out many times a day whenever it rains or the wind blows. Now there is a major wind storm, so we will be powerless for the next few hours.

Sometimes it's the Little Things; 6-24-14

Grace and mercy can be extended at times and from places you least expect. God is surely looking out for us. He surely hasn't forgotten us yet.

We have an awesome grocery shop here in the city called Easy Way. It is actually owned by the mighty Wal-Mart. It basically has the same things that you would find at a Dollar General or Family Dollar in the United States with the inclusion of produce and frozen items. I buy a lot of my personal supplies there. The staff is super friendly and know me by name. A few months ago, I invited a couple of workers to come visit us. They obliged and also brought some rice for the boys.

Yesterday, as I was leaving the shop, I noticed they had purged their produce for the day and it was in a couple of small shopping carts next the dumpster out front. I asked the manager what he did with the day-old produce and he said they either toss it or give it to the sacred cows. Even in India they are throwing away day-old produce!!!

I asked him if he would give it to our orphans because I think they are sacred and we would really like all of the fresh vegetables. He asked me if I was sure. The truth is, the vegetables we can buy here in our small village outside of the city are actually worse looking than the ones he was about to throw away. I imagine that our vegetables here in our village are probably a week past their prime, not a day. I told him that it was a blessing for him to give the food to our boys and he agreed. I already bought so much before noticing this that I didn't have enough space on my motorcycle to carry it. I asked him when we could come by again and he told me to come at 11 a.m. the next day. That was this morning. Around 11 a.m., I was knee-deep in problems here. Our power keeps surging and going out, and the pump for our well finally died. I was busy trying to get an electrician to come here and fix the problem. Needless to say, the time slipped by me and I didn't even notice.

At 12 p.m., I got a call on my cell. I thought it was the electrician. It wasn't. It was the produce man from Easy Way. He was calling to ask me if I was coming. I told him I would be there as soon as I possibly could.

The cool thing was that I hadn't given him my number. To my knowledge, no one at the store has it. He called around to other shopkeepers until he found someone who knew me and acquired my number from him. He tracked me down and took the time to call and let me know he had saved the veggies for us.

When I got there, I was pleasantly surprised. I am not really sure exactly how much was there, but I would estimate that it was a good fifty pounds, divided into two large potato sacks that I had to bring back on my bike. Nicodemus went with me, so he had a twenty-five pound bag in his lap while I balanced the second bag on my gas tank and between my handlebars. I had to drive very slow and still had a few "close encounters of the Indian traffic kind."

The best part is that the manager came out and told me he is willing to give us the produce every day if we are willing to come get it. I am glad the regulations for this kind of thing are different than they are in the United States; otherwise, I doubt we could jump through the paperwork hoops to get it done. Even if this is a short-term kind of thing, I am blessed and happy to know we have new friends looking out for us and that our boys will get some great veggies at a pleasant price :)
Here is a list of what we received:

cilantro

tomatoes

capsicum

potatoes

gourd

mangoes

pumpkins

okra

cucumbers

lemons

7/31/2014

Eating a meal at Hotel Shoran. We had to bring the boys and staff in four trips. The boys have been studying hard and working hard. There are a lot of chores to do around our twenty acres and 20,000 square foot building. Today was a holiday from school, so I bit the grocery budget bullet and decided to reward them with dinner outside. Most of the boys have never eaten out. I will figure out our food pantry next week. God is great.

Addition and Subtraction = I HATE MATH! 8/04/14

I hate math. I always have. Just ask Clayton King. He says math is of the devil. He says that "God is not the author of confusion. Math is confusing, therefore if math is confusing and God didn't create it, it must be of the devil." He definitely has a point. Actually, I love addition and multiplication. I just don't like subtraction or division, or any of the rest of it.

This is what I mean: For the summer, we had three of our boys go home for vacation. I waited patiently for them to return. It just didn't feel the same without them. I truly could hear three less laughs during our play times. I felt three less hugs every Sunday morning after our worship service was over. There were three less bodies running around and I could feel it in my heart.

School started on July 2nd and they had not returned yet. I was really getting worried. On the 4th, I came back from the vegetable market and they were there sitting under our neem tree. There mothers were there also. When I saw them, I felt that everything would return to normal, but I was wrong. Their mothers had decided to remove them from our care and have them back at home. They were coming to withdraw from school and to gather their things. My emotions were so mixed that I still haven't come to grips with them yet. I mean, on one side I was so happy they would be at home with their mothers. There is no alternative to a mother's love, but I was also deeply saddened firstly because their mothers are very poor and have no jobs. What kind of life will my boys have? What will they eat? Secondly, they were being removed from school with no plan to go back. What will become of them? I feared they would continue in the never-ending cycle of poverty just like their parents and their parents' parents. Education is the only way to break the cycle. I was also distraught because these are my boys. They call me Papa. Their own fathers had either died or ran away, and I stepped in and took the title seriously. I love them as my own. I would willingly give my life for them, and here they are saying goodbye. It's been a month and I haven't heard from them. Honestly, I don't know if I ever will. God allowed me to have a special bond with them that will never be replaced. I don't want it to. I cry when I remember them. I grieve.

Fast forward to yesterday. I had been in talks with a local pastor that knew of three brothers that needed a home. Their parents are very poor and cannot take care of them. I guided the pastor through the paperwork we needed in order to take the boys in. Yesterday, the three brothers arrived. It was emotional watching them have to say goodbye to their father. They were confused, dejected, and I can only imagine that they felt abandoned.

It wasn't long before the other boys had taken them under their wing. The others boys told them stories about me and assured them that everything would be okay. They sheepishly called me "Papa" also, even though I am sure they find it a little weird. Today, they hit the ground running and you would never be able to tell tell that they haven't been here for years. They are just one of my boys. They are tender hearted, feisty, and protective of each other. Just like me.

So I lost three boys and gained three boys within a month. I feel a bit like Job. To be honest, I have never fully understood some people's interpretation of what happened to Job. I mean, I know what happened and I believe it. He lost all of his sons and daughters. Then, in the end, he was given back the same amount of sons and daughters and increased in other ways also.

The part that always gets me is that even though he was given seven sons and three daughters in the end, how could it ever replace the heartache of losing the first ten? There is no way it can. If I lose my house, I can build again. If I lose a child, I will never be the same. Even though Job was "restored", I don't think he ever forgot the first of his children. It is made to seem that he had ten children, when in reality he had twenty. ten perished, and ten were alive.

This is how I feel. My heart is on my sleeve. I am rejoicing that today I have three new sons. But they do not replace three that I lost. They are in addition to the three I lost. Counting the twenty-eight boys we currently have, I am a Papa of thirty-one boys. I will miss you Ronnie, Asher, and Reuben. I will always be your Papa. My heart is big enough for them all. Soon, we will have one hundred boys and they are each special, even my three new boys, Thomas, Abel, and Eustace.

Little "Mark" joins us; 8/14/2014

My heart is a little overwhelmed. Here is our newest boy.
He is three. I cannot imagine being that young and being left
behind. My heart melts at the thought of him crying for his mother
tonight. I put him in my bed sound asleep. He promptly peed
everywhere. That's ok. I love him anyway. Please pray for his little
sweet heart, as the next few days will surely be very hard.

Birthday Bread; 8/22/14

We just celebrated the 2nd annual Best Birthday Party Ever! It was amazing. Please understand that we are in a constant battle between spending money on what is absolutely necessary and occasionally spending money to establish memories for these boys. Although it may sound controversial, birthday parties are not a necessity of life, however, the memories created are priceless. Our budget was virtually nothing for the party. We used old decorations. I bought the boys an inexpensive DVD player and actually put their current TV in a box to make it look bigger.

They either didn't notice or didn't care. They were just happy to have a party. It took me days to plan and coordinate, and hours to decorate. Bear in mind that we only have a few staff members and they didn't quite get the idea when I shared it with them. They thought it was a waste of resources. I mean, we have so many things to do, why spend it on a party? Truthfully, the actual party didn't cost a whole lot and I bought the gifts from my own pocket. Their gift bags included a new pair of shoes and a new shirt. Have you ever bought shoes and shirts for thirty-six boys at one fell swoop? That was intense. I gave the boys marbles and kites also. The total cost of the kite and marbles was five cents per boy. I bought a few collective sporting items for everyone to share like a couple of soccer balls, cricket bats, and a small basketball hoop.

One of the weirdest gifts I have ever given was a loaf of bread. A couple of weeks ago, a local businessman came by and provided a meal for the boys. At the end, he gave them ten rupees each to use at their school canteen. The next day, about half of the boys brought me their ten rupees and asked if I would go buy them a loaf of bread each. Ten rupees is about sixteen cents. I laughed. Trust me, these boys eat good food, but if that's what they want to spend their money on, I have no problem with it. So I went out and bought the bread. They all shared it and thoroughly enjoyed it. Well, when I was thinking of good things to add to their birthday bag, I immediately thought of the bread. So, I bought forty loaves of bread and added them to the bags. The funny thing is that when I was passing out their bags to them, the thought of getting bread made them giddy. They grabbed the bread and dropped the rest of the things. They didn't even look at what color shoes they got or the style of their new shirt. They were just so excited to get bread! It reminds me of children who get expensive toys and end up playing with the box on Christmas morning. What a hoot!

As I was running around like a crazy person just minutes before the party, a mother brought her two sons to be admitted. She had all the paperwork. I paused what I was doing and gave her my full attention. The two boys were a bit terrified. Knowing that the huge party was just minutes away, and we had no clue they were coming, we rushed out to buy shoes and shirts and make them a part of the party. The oldest boy was visibly shaken and didn't want his mother to leave; both of the boys automatically knew that this is a home of love. They both embraced me and gave me looks that they knew we would take great care of them. They immediately called me Papa and seemed to loosen up. I insisted on their mother staying for the start of the party where we blew out the candles on the cake. This is where every boy gets a candle to blow out. For some reason, I bought two cakes, but it all was soon about to make sense. As a staff member was talking to the mother, we found out that it was the oldest boy's birthday. What amazing timing! He never had a birthday party before, and he just walked into the greatest birthday party ever, and I had an extra cake! Before we even started the party, I had him come up and we sang "Happy Birthday" as he blew out the candle.

After the gifts were given, we all danced and sang to Bollywood music and had a blast. We then played all the sports and ate the snack trays I had assembled with six different goodies.

We had an amazing time. I cannot compare it to last year because that was a one in a lifetime event. After doing a headcount, we discovered that almost half of our current boys have come since last year. They experienced something like that for the first time and that's what makes it so special.

A staff member came up to me during the party and told me that this was one of the greatest things he had ever seen. He said he was sorry for thinking it was a waste of money. He told me that money cannot buy happiness, but this party made the boys the happiest he had seen. Bread seems to have the power to do that to my boys :)

Cluck! Cluck! Cluck! 8/31/14

The chickens are coming! The chickens are coming! One if by car, two if by truck. The chickens are coming, the chickens are coming. I assume you have read all about the Chicken Challenge. This is a simple update.

We have found it rather hard to find 300 chickens for sale around here. We can't just go to Hen-Mart or Chickens-R-Us. It takes a long time to go farmer to farmer trying to find "desi" chickens. Desi is the Hindi word meaning local. Although we will continue to search for as many grown hens or pullets that we can find, we are not sitting around and waiting. We are being proactive.

After doing some internet research, I sought out some local hatcheries. Although they do not sell full grown chickens without purchasing them months in advance, they do sell day-old chicks, or DOC. The cost of a DOC is drastically lower than a full hen, but it is not without its risks. Having a proper place to raise the chicks is crucial. They require vaccinations and costly feed to start their life. They require brooders which are basically light and heating sources. Also, you hope and pray they don't die before they are full-grown. If they reach maturity, you have saved a good amount over buying a laying hen.

I have put in an order at two different hatcheries. The first was for one hundred normal Indian broiler chicks. They grow fast and are meant for meat only. They will not lay eggs. They are lazy and make me sad. Honestly, their quality of life just isn't good.

The second order is what I am more excited about. We have ordered 500 DOC of a new breed of chickens called Kuroilers. They were bred to be both meat and egg laying chickens. They were bred to be disease resistant, easy to take care of, and hard to accidentally kill. They were bred to run away from predators unlike the dumb chickens we currently have that want to make friends with the random dogs. These Kuroilers were also bred to be able to eat almost anything and to live off the land and not eat as much feed. This will help us keep our costs down. Most Indians prefer to eat roosters, so our goal is to raise the rooster chicks to be either sold for meat or eaten by us while we will raise our hens to lay eggs. The ratio of hens to roosters is about 60%-40% so at the end of our forty-five days, we will have sold off or eaten 200 roosters and have 300 new females that will eventually lay eggs. This number, of course, doesn't include the 100 white normal chickens that we just picked up. We will sell or eat all of these within the next thirty-five to forty days. I will do a blog about the Kuroilers once I pick them up in a couple of weeks.

Until then, I want to boast about our new 100 DOC. They are bright yellow but will soon lose the baby fuzz and grow white feathers. They are so cute at this point. The boys are having a blast, but I have made it extremely clear why we are raising these chicks. I told the boys that these chicks are not like the other thirty chickens outside. The chickens outside are meant only for eggs so they will be with us for a long time, but these chicks are meant only to raise and eat. They are not meant to be pets, and we shouldn't give them names (they all look the same anyway-how could you tell who is who). The boys understand about life and death on our farm. We have had many chickens die. We have lost many puppies through the years because of many reasons. They may not understand fully about life and death, but they have experienced it. Let us know what you think of our pretty little chicks.

Canteen; 8/31/14

We have opened a canteen at the orphanage. The boys can take a plethora of stuff, but it's probably not what you think. Our boys are hard workers. They do well in school, they are polite and diligent, and they are devoted. They even take chore time serious.

A few weeks ago, a local businessman from outside brought lunch for the boys. As he was leaving, he asked if it was okay to give every boy ten rupees, which is sixteen cents. I said it was fine. Later I asked JP, my best friend and our home director, what the boys could possibly use it for. It's not like I wanted to take the money since it was a gift to them, but it's also not like they have a lot of places to spend money. JP told me that they would use it at the school canteen. I have to be honest, I had no idea what he was talking about. School canteen? It seems as though there is a canteen at their school where they can buy cookies, fruit juice, pencils, erasers, etc.

My first thought was a little bit of shame. The boys had never mentioned this to me, and I had no clue. Even though I am at their school a lot, I have never noticed the canteen. I was saddened at the thought of my boys daily having free time but not being able to make these simple purchases like the other boys. I felt bad at the thought of them feeling different because they could not take part.

I decided to give them an allowance for all of the hard work they do. Their allowance would be forty rupees per week and they would have chances periodically to gain extra money. Forty rupees is roughly seventy-five cents. My first thought was to give them the cash on Monday morning before school and let them do with it as they wish. I quickly changed my mind when I thought of a better way. Just giving people cash does no good without education. In fact, it may be detrimental. The last thing I want to do to my boys is create in them the propensity to misuse money. It's not like seventy-five cents will change their world if misused, but this could be a simple learning opportunity that will stay with them for a lifetime.

I decided to create a canteen here at Shiloh. I filled it with crackers, nuts, and fruit juices. I added marbles, school supplies, and kites. I told the boys that the canteen had the ability to order anything they wanted. If they wanted new shoes, we could purchase them. The key is that they would be spending their own money.

The same day we decided to do the canteen, I gave the boys the chance to earn some money by walking and running for charity. Friends of ours are adopting a boy internationally and were doing a virtual 5k. The boys signed up and I committed to give them one rupee for every lap they went. I knew this would be a good start to the canteen. Little did I realize how serious they would take it. The winning boy ran 640 laps in two days, which is a total of thirty two miles! The boy with the lowest total had 250 laps.

This was a good start to the canteen. I have seen the boys in a different way than before. At first, there were no restrictions and some boys would spend fifty rupees per day. I quickly changed the rule that the maximum anyone could spend per day was twenty rupees. I noticed that even though some boys could spend the twenty rupees, they were satisfied with only using five rupees for a pack of crackers, or didn't buy anything at all. I asked one boy why he didn't buy more, and he said he was saving to buy some nicer shoes. The boys do get new shoes occasionally, but he knew exactly the ones he wanted and is willing to save up.

The canteen has some pretty simple rules. It is open for only a few minutes in the middle of the afternoon, so it doesn't affect their lunch or dinner. The boys are to stand in an orderly line and wait patiently for their turn. If you cut in line, you may lose your privileges for the day. They are encouraged to make wise choices. A pack of cookies is okay; four packages is not. They can spend a max of twenty rupees per day, which can be up to four items depending on the price. Once they choose their items, I "ring" them up. I have a page for every boy in my logbook . On their page, I write down the date, the items they buy, the cost, and then I require them to sign their name. By signing their name, they are taking ownership. They are not allowed to dawdle and hover. They must leave the canteen at once and wait for their friends outside. Although I love them as only a Papa does, I treat them as if I am a store owner and they are valued customers. I believe they appreciate this interaction.

I have had to close the canteen down a few times because the boys used their wrappers to litter. They are learning that even though almost no one else here cares about litter, we do, because this is our home and we take pride in it. The boys understand that although this is something they earn, it can also be taken away if they do not behave properly.

One of my goals coming up is to give the boys the ability to use some of their canteen money to buy baby chicks. They will be responsible for raising them and feeding them for thirty to thirty-five days. They will reap the benefits whenever we sell the bird for meat, or I buy it from them to feed the home. I am almost giddy at the idea of teaching them how, if they use their money wisely, they can increase it. There is, of course, the chance for baby chicks to die, not put on enough weight, etc. If they are willing to take a calculated risk, they can turn their allowance into a salary of sorts.

Our canteen is not much. It has bread, nuts, fruit, and marbles. Most everything costs about five rupees each. However, you cannot put a price tag on the life lesson it is teaching my boys.

Meet Wally; 10/07/14

This is not an easy story to tell, but it needs to be told. For safety reasons, we have changed this boy's name in this story to Walrus, or Wally. Wally is twelve years old. Wally's' father lost his mother in a gambling debt - a card game gone wrong. I wish this was a fictional story, but it is not.

His father truly lost his mother in a drunken card game. His mother was now indebted to and had to leave with another man. When his father came out of his drunken, high stupor, he realized what he had done. He did the only thing a coward knows how to do. He took it out on Wally. He beat him so severely that he cracked and broke Wally's skull. You read that right. The father beat his own son so badly that HE BROKE HIS SKULL!!!! I am crying just thinking about it. Wally was knocked unconscious and drifted in and out of consciousness for the next two days. His mother waited for two days before she built up enough courage to run away from her new "man." She ran to the police who also brought in social workers. They went to the home and found Wally and his brother. Wally was admitted into the hospital and slipped into a coma for a month. That was honestly the safest place he could be. After he came to, he, his mother, and his brother stayed at a battered women's shelter, but it was only temporary. The police and the social workers brought the two brothers to us. His mother was also there. It was emotional. The boys did not want to leave their mother. The younger brother quickly assimilated and was having fun in no time. But Wally was not happy. In fact, after his mother left, he cried uncontrollably and cut his arm. He would have done anything to have his mother come and take him away. I sat with him and held him. I didn't talk too much, tell him that things were better, or that this was happening for a purpose. I just simply held onto him, and he clung to me.

I have an advantage. When new boys come to us, the last thing they want is for someone to replace their mother and father. They have a hard time opening up to the other staff. However, since I am a big white teddy bear figure, most cling to me. They do not see me as a threat to replace their father.

Wally stayed by my side for the first month. It was not a fun month. When I took him to school to be admitted and placed, they informed me that he was previously in eighth grade. He was first in his class and hadn't made a B in two years. When they tested him, because of his brain injury, he couldn't even recite the alphabet. They had no choice but to place him in Kindergarten. Here was a twelve-year-old boy who had lost his mother; his father had brutally beaten him, had no home, was in a new environment, and was now having to deal with his brain injury by having to start school ALL OVER AGAIN!

It was not pleasant, to say the least. He felt different, strange, and awkward. He was embarrassed. When he first arrived, I could tell that he was dealing with a head injury. He would stare off into space and be zoned out. Many times, he would tell me that his brain felt like a cloud. This poor boy was facing every uphill battle imaginable.

We simply loved him through it. I am not here to say that he is completely well. He is not. He is still dealing with abandonment issues. His brother adjusted the moment he arrived, but Wally still feels awkward and out of place. He knows he doesn't think or act like the other boys his age, but he knows that he is loved. He is beginning to adjust and come out of the fog and cloud he has from his PTSD and brain injury. I will continue to be there with him every step of the way, holding him tight, and letting him cling to me. He is still on the way up the hill, but he is doing better. That's what I live for.

You see, this is why we do what we do. We stand in the gap for these precious little boys and young men when the world discards them. We are there to pick them up and protect them when the world abuses and beats them. It's what we are called to do. We have been uniquely equipped by God for this. It is the essence of who we are. Seeing the small strides like Wally has made in such a short time gives us the resolve to keep fighting.

We have added fourteen boys in a one-month span. Many have similar stories to Wally's. Their arrival has destroyed our budget. We are at the end of our financial rope. These aren't case studies for us. They are not distant stories we have heard. This is real life for us. To see one of these boys rebound the way Wally has makes this whole thing worthwhile. It's a life worth fighting for, even when we don't know where the next support will come from.

There are countless boys and girls outside of our door with stories like Wally. We don't have the budget to support them, but God does. We firmly believe that if He sends them our way, He will also send the people to partner with us. That makes me feel loved in a way that I try to show the boys.

We took a first picture of Wally. If you saw it, you would notice the blank stare and the emotion and hurt behind the eyes. It was taken one month later. It is of the same boy who now feels loved, secure, and safe. This is what No Longer Orphans does for these boys. Thank you for remembering us in prayer and for considering supporting us as God leads you.

Hair Today, Gone Tomorrow; 11/05/14

I previously sent out a challenge that if we raised enough funds, I would allow the boys to cut my hair. That was a bad idea on my part. It's not like I was gaining any beauty points for my current hair fashion statement, so for the sake of the challenge, I grew it super long. I looked like a cross between a blonde Ronald McDonald and a fat Carrot Top. I grew my beard out, too. Susan was in the United States for two months, so that is the only way I could pull this off. Otherwise, she would not have let it go that far, even for a challenge. Long story short, we reached our goal and the boys shaved my head.

In fact, my sister is part of our Virtual Family program and she and her kids communicate with "Amos". When I recently posted a PhotoShopped picture of my sister, she took it upon herself to one-up me. She made up the difference that we needed for the challenge on the condition that Amos could be the one who shaved my head at the end…and shave my head he did! Anyway, the boys had a blast cutting my hair. I was hot and miserable, and it wasn't my best day, but the video is real, and we were all being ourselves.

Do me a favor though, if you feel led - please make a donation so I don't have to do this again :) My scalp can only take so much.

My 38th birthday; 11-07-14

The boys have surprised me by taking me out to dinner at a restaurant with a discotheque in the basement. Good times.

Some funny sentences from the forty birthday cards from the boys:

"Papa, I hope that you are thirty-eight years old. "

"God gave you a good life."

"God blessy."

"I pary for you."

"Papa, one story for you called Jingle Bells. Dashing through the snow on a one horse open sleigh. (he then writes out the whole song)

"Good bless you Papa"

"may God give you everlasting life"

"Happy Papa, birthday"

*One boy colored me fourteen pictures

*All the Christmas cards sent last year have seemed to have been recycled.

*One boy took a blank Christmas card and wrote his name inside with nothing else.

*One boy glued my business card to the outside of his card.

I am just overwhelmed. These boys are so creative and they try their best. God does have a sense of humor, and I think He allows me to have some of these funny moments to keep me energized. I truly believe the boys value my birthday because I value their birthday. Last night, I went out with Sanjay for his birthday and he was the happiest kid alive. No one could have wiped the smile off his face. None of them had ever experienced that kind of joy before. I am doing nothing special, simply doing for them what my family did for me - having a day when you are special and treated like a king, a day where "it's your day, it's your way." Of course, this isn't totally uncommon for India, but it is unheard of for poor street orphans that were struggling to get by just a few short months ago. I value my birthday not for myself, but for the growth and joy that I see present in my forty sons.

11/29/2014

Even in the midst of our hardships, God shows up. Today, in between visits by government officials, we put up some Christmas decorations. Now the boys are signing all of your Christmas cards. It's been a very rough week. A group of boys were standing under the decorations and belly laughing. They all said, "Papa, Christmas is coming!" None of these boys were with us last year, and it hit me hard that this is the first Christmas they have ever had. Makes a grown man get choked up thinking about it. After a week of fighting with people who would rather see us close up and these boys back on the streets, it's overwhelming when God shows up. This is why we do what we do.

12/31/2014

Our fireworks were so bright and plentiful that the police and firetrucks came because they thought our building was on fire.

Christmas Bikes for the Boys; 1/07/15

In the unforgettable words of the one and only Pee Wee Herman, "What's missing from this picture?? It's just me, without my bike!!!"

Do you remember the Christmas when you got your first bike? You had a feeling that you could take on the world. Nothing could stop you. The joy and excitement of that Christmas is one you will never, ever forget. You have the opportunity to give the same gift of excitement by donating.

I question the authenticity of a childhood that didn't involve a bike. Well, not really, but bicycles at their essence scream, "childhood memories." I remember one time on Arrowhead Drive where my friends and I made a makeshift ramp and we jumped it until the sun went down every day. It was all fun and games when we had a brick as the height. However, the day I removed the brick and added a cinder block, everything changed. I hit the ramp at full speed and was propelled a lot farther than I had calculated, which sent me over the handlebars when I touched down. I still have the scars over thirty years later. Good times, good times.

Or the time that we lived by Long Pond in Lake Park and my mother worked extra shifts for a month to buy me a new bike.

We were pretty poor at the time and I wasn't expecting it. I loved that bike. It was my first bike with gears. We moved shortly after that, and I started a new school within walking distance of our house. I drove my bike to school one day and forgot to lock it when I went in for band practice. Needless to say, it was stolen. I felt horrible that I hadn't locked it, and felt even worse when I thought about all those hours my mother worked to get me that bike.

That story isn't meant to leave a bad taste in your mouth. I am sure we all have some kind of bike story from our childhood. It's just a part of growing up.

The joys of bicycles are not lost on Indian kids, and surely not my orphan boys. They know what joys lie in the ownership of a bike. At their school, roughly 200 children ride their bikes to school daily (I wish we still did that in the United States). They see the freedom and joy on the faces of their friends and they want to feel that also.

Last year for Christmas, I bought two bikes for the orphanage. One was meant to do local errands. It was bulky and had a huge basket on the front. The second one was for the older boys. I was wrong in thinking that only the older boys would want to ride it. They ALL wanted to ride it and everyone tried. The very small kids couldn't reach, but for the medium-sized kids their feet just fit. "Zachary" was a little on the small size, but that didn't stop him. Although both of his feet didn't fit, one of his feet could reach the pedal at its highest point, so he would ride it one-footed and kick off with all his might when that pedal rolled around.

110

Even today, when there is daily free time, there is a line of about ten boys patiently waiting their turn to ride our single bike. I want this Christmas to be a little different. My desire and goal is to provide an opportunity for every boy to take ownership of their own bike, including the maintenance. If there are needed repairs, the boys will be required to pay for them from their canteen money.

First ,we need to buy the bikes. Won't you help? The cost of each bike is forty four dollars. We need a total of forty bikes. Please take a moment to change the childhood of an orphan boy today.

NOTE: The follow up blog post:

If you follow us on Facebook, you may have seen the fulfillment of our Secret Santa Bike Challenge. It was an overwhelming success! It was an amazing day that we will not soon forget. The children were totally surprised and overwhelmed to get such a wonderful gift. They had no clue that they would each get a bike!

On December 23, "Santa" showed up, danced with the children, sang songs before he passed out candy, and disappeared into the night. An hour later, the boys were given what they thought was their only Christmas gift. We gave them a steel foot locker filled with clothes, small toys, snacks and candy. They had no clue that this wasn't their gift, but merely their "stocking."

It is our personal tradition here at Shiloh that we give no gifts on Christmas Day. I want that day to be a day of reflection and concentrating on the reason for the season.   So, on December

26, it was time. We waited until the boys were having morning prayer and we wheeled all forty bikes out into the main hall.

After everything was set up we encouraged the boys to finish their time and come see what was in store. The boys flooded out of the room and had differing but awesome reactions. Some stood in awe with their mouths gaping open. Some boys rushed to the bicycles like their pants were on fire. Some boys rushed over to me and hugged me with all their might shouting, "Thank you Papa!!" It was an amazing time, and the boys continue to thoroughly enjoy their bikes.

Every Kid Deserves a Shot; 1/21/15 (written by Dr Stephen Renfrow)

Introduction: Stephen Renfrow is a Pediatrician at Charlotte Pediatric Clinic. He is a long time supporter of No Longer Orphans. We count him as a dear friend and advisor for the children's health needs. He is one of the funniest people I have ever known, a die-hard Carolina Panthers fan, and an amazing father. He truly fights for children daily and can be seen some weekends running charity races for adoptions or children's needs. Please take the time to read his guest blog below about the importance of vaccinations in India, and every child in developing nations. — Andy Lepper

Guest Post by Dr. Renfrow: While medical records may be lacking somewhat, I am told that none of the boys at Shiloh have ever had vaccines. NONE. EVER. While that is not an entirely surprising reality in India, it is still pretty hard for us to fathom. Sure, there are some kids in the States that don't have all their vaccines, but those are primarily due to parental choice not to vaccinate rather than a true lack of access to these vaccines. We often take things like vaccines for granted since they are such a routine part of pediatric healthcare here in the United States, but the truth is many children around the world aren't so fortunate.

Over the last two decades, vaccination has helped cut childhood deaths in half, but the stark reality remains that an estimated 1.5 million children under age five still die each year from diseases that could have been prevented by vaccines. That is absolutely staggering to me. It's just not acceptable, and by that, I mean we should refuse to accept it.

Along with clean water and sanitation, immunization is one of the most cost-effective public health investments ever. EVER. In a nutshell, here's how vaccines work: A harmless form of a virus or bacterium is introduced the immune system, and the healthy immune system recognizes this antigen as something that doesn't belong. It therefore creates antibodies or defenses to this virus or bacterium so that if it is ever encountered again, the body will be able to protect and defend itself. It's sort of more complicated than that, but honestly, it's just that simple. And here's the thing, it works. Vaccines used today are both safe and effective. They are EXTENSIVELY studied and researched, and they save lives.

According to UNICEF, 70% of the unvaccinated children in the world live in just ten countries. Those countries are the Democratic Republic of Congo, Ethiopia, Indonesia, Iraq, Nigeria, Pakistan, the Philippines, Uganda, South Africa, and...well, you guessed it...India. Without access to these routine childhood vaccines, pneumococcal disease (a bacteria that can cause pneumonia, meningitis, and bloodstream infections) kills an estimated 476,000 kids EVERY YEAR and rotavirus (a viral diarrhea) kills an estimated 453,000 kids EVERY YEAR. Measles kills another 118,00 kids per year. These are OUR kids. These kids are the future of our world. Kids made in the image of God, just like the kids in our country, and just like the kids in our own homes. Here's the heartbreaking part: most of these deaths are easily preventable with access to vaccines. These precious children don't have to die.

Even if you were a heartless jerk and didn't care about kids (which I'm pretty sure you DO care if you're reading this), vaccines make sense from a cost perspective. If vaccination programs in the world's poorest seventy-two countries were brought up to speed, over the next decade the cost savings to the world is estimated (by UNICEF again) to be as high as $6.2 billion in treatment costs. Yep. That would be BILLION with a B.

It works that way on a smaller scale too. It is much most cost-effective for the Shiloh boys to be vaccinated against these preventable illness than it would be to cover the cost of their care if they got sick and/or hospitalized. It just makes sense...and cents (sorry, I couldn't help it). Combine this cost-effectiveness with the fact that every kid deserves to be healthy and free of disease, and hopefully you'll see that vaccinating these boys should be a no-brainer.

Please know that your donations to No Longer Orphans go towards paying for very real tangible things like vaccines. You're not paying for an idea or a cause. You are very likely buying the very pneumococcal vaccine or the measles vaccine that will keep one of these boys out of the hospital or possibly even keep them from an early, preventable death. These aren't nameless faces. You can click over to another page on this site and look at each of their faces and read each of names RIGHT NOW. This stuff matters. We serve a mighty God who loves each one of these boys, and I think it is amazing that we get to play even a small part of keeping them healthy and happy.

(All the statistics in this post came from www.unicefusa.org. This information is easily available to anyone with internet access who wants to read and learn more. I am a big proponent of folks educating themselves with good, true, verified information. Knowledge is power.)

Animal Appreciation   2/04/15

This month, February, is Animal Appreciation Month. We will spend the month sharing with you all of the awesome things that animals have meant to our orphanage and to the boys in general. We will have a couple of blogs by animal lovers who have agreed to contribute. Since the introduction of animals here at the orphanage, they have become a huge part of our daily life.

Last month was Health Awareness Month. We had a great guest blog by Dr. Stephen Renfrow. Thank you for bearing with us as we establish this awareness month concept. We did not post as many blogs as we anticipated because I had a health scare myself and was out of action for a couple of weeks. Life happens.

You may wonder why we need so many animals. The first reason is very simple: sustainability. We survive on the donations of kind folks like yourself. Most of the donations come when people read our blogs, feel a connection, and are compelled to help us meet our needs. But the truth is, we do not get very many donations outside of designated projects like this. So there are months when we have very little in our general budget and have to make tough choices. We pride ourselves on integrity, so when someone donates to a specific project, 100% of their money goes to that project. PERIOD. It is not held in case we come up short with our general budget. When we do come up short, first and foremost is food for the children. When there is a deficit, they still eat a healthy well-balanced diet like normal. Next in line is their health, then comes school, and on down the line. The truth is that some months we come up a little short in paying salary, school fees, hygiene, budget, or whatever is last in line.

The animals are a way for us to be self-sufficient here in case of months where the funding is lacking. Our goal is to sell chickens, eggs, and milk from the water buffalos, cows, and goats along with meat from goats. This will help us to provide extraordinary care for these precious boys. Our ultimate goal is to be totally sufficient one day. We have the desire to take in and care for 150 boys total. That means an increase of 110 more boys. I don't like thinking how it will be to provide for 150 when we can barely feed forty some months, but there is hope. By adding animals, we will be able to naturally increase our numbers and provide them with everything they need to grow, learn, and live.

The second reason we want so many animals is because after we are sustainable we want to be a blessing for other orphanages. No Longer Orphans is the sole supporter of the Shiloh Orphanage, but we also want to help out others when and where we can. We have a network of over 100 orphanages with almost 10,000 children. Many of them do not even have enough resources to provide healthy daily food requirements. We know some orphanages who feed only rice to their children for every meal. We want to be part of the solution. We can donate some of the offspring to other orphanages by breeding the purchased animals. We plan to hatch thousands of chickens every year that we can donate to other orphanages and at-risk women to help provide eggs and meat for their children.

Those are the two main reasons we want to purchase the animals we have listed. Our goal is to be sustainable within five years through this animal initiative. Your donation of any amount is multiplied exponentially. Your donation of a chicken is multiplied when you factor in that the chickens we raise will lay about 500 eggs in their lifetime. If we were to take just 10% of those, hatch them, and continue to do so, your donation of one chicken could potentially be a donation of 5,000 chickens within a few years. Here is the breakdown of what the current cost of each animal is.

- Four-week old chicks: $1 each
- Ducks: $5 each
- 1 Water buffalo with calf: $800
- 1 Jersey Cow with calf: $800
- 1 Goat: $100

Please prayerfully consider donating to the animal fund: https://nlorphans.nationbuilder.com/donate_animal_fund

Also, please keep checking in to see some of our fun updates about our wild and zany animals in the next few weeks.

You do WHAT with the water buffalo poop?????; 2/12/15

Here is another entry for the Animal Appreciation Month. What do we do with all the poop that our buffalos create?

We have two water buffaloes, and, boy do they poop. A lot! Here in India, it's not just used as fertilizer. It has another strange use. People actually use buffalo and cow dung to cook with! They mix the fresh dung with water and pound it out in the shape of a patty and leave it out to dry. Drying it out removes almost all of the smell and moisture. People use it as fuel for a fire so they can cook.

We sell our buffalo patties to local village people for them to use for cooking. This may sound utterly disgusting, but it's just part of life here in an Indian village. We do not personally cook with it. I would rather buy wood. The reason people use it is because it is very cheap and abundant.

We do not make a whole lot from the sale of our buffalo dung, but it is just another way that we are moving towards sustainability. Nothing goes to waste.

If you want to help us buy a few more water buffalos and cows, please donate to our animal fund.

https://nlorphans.nationbuilder.com/donate_animal_fund

Chicken or the Egg; 2/13/15

Who cares what came first! Here at the orphanage, we just care that both the egg and the chicken are here to stay! Both are quite delicious. We want to share with you all the glory that is our wonderful chickens. I will share with you more about our chickens than anyone could ever possibly care about.

We currently have hundreds of chickens. Half of those we have raised since they were a day old. The other half of our chicken we bought as pullets (teenage chickens:) We got them when they were ten weeks old. The older birds have just started laying and we are getting about fifty eggs per day. This has been a huge blessing for us. We give the boys eggs every other day and sell the rest. It took us months of careful diets to get there so we are very excited to be recouping some of the investment we have in the chickens.

So what do we feed the chickens? First thing in the morning, we jump start their day by giving them a mix we grind from scratch. For the younger chickens, it includes dent corn, wheat, rice, bajra (which is a small Indian corn), guar, and a grower pellet. For the older birds, we give pretty much the same mix but use a layer pellet instead of the grower pellet. The awesome part is we grow everything on our land except for the pellets. We grow the corn, wheat, bajra, and guar. We mill it on site, too. We even make our own wheat flour and corn flour.

For lunch, we give the chickens a bountiful supply of fresh cut grass and veggies, about one hundred pounds of it. We actually have a field of grass raised exclusively for the animals. We also receive vegetables donated from a local store. After we pick out the best produce for the children, we give the rest to the chickens. For the grass, Dale runs the long grass through our grass cutting machine. Think of it as a heavy vertical lawn mower. Dale even cuts wild mustard greens and stalks that we found growing wild in our grass fields.

Finally, I want to share with you the latest addition to our chicken yard. At night, we have big chicken coops covered with tarps where the chickens sleep. I wanted to provide something nice and cool during the day so they could be comfortable when laying their eggs. We had some old iron beds that are broken and too big for the boys. I turned eight of them on their sides and constructed a fort. We lined two beds per side and then covered the top with a tarp. I inserted a post in the center as a way to let the rain run off. Each bed has an upper and lower section where four hens can lay comfortably on each level or get out of the sweltering Indian heat. In case you weren't aware, our city has the highest recorded temperature in India. We have dubbed the chicken fort as the New Murghi Mahal. Murghi is the Hindi word for chicken. The hens have taken to it already and we are now finding most of the eggs they lay are in the NMM.

Thank you for taking the time to read about our chickens here on our orphan farm. If you want to be a part of what we are doing, please consider donating to our animal fund.

Did you eat Minnie Mouse??? 2/24/15 (written by Kimberly Morgan, one of our supporters)

Kimberly Morgan is one of my favorite friends. She and I were awkward teenagers that struck up an unlikely friendship. She is married to an incredibly awesome purple-hearted Marine who serves our country well. She has lived in Japan and has a true love for culture. She has been researching local African American history for about a decade to help preserve the legacy (and history) of a few local families. She is real, compassionate, and hilarious. She is also a huge animal lover. She works and volunteers at her local veterinary clinic. She loves animals more than anyone I know, and I asked her to write a blog post on what animals mean to her. I hope you enjoy reading this as much as I have. - Andy

"DROP THE MINNIE MOUSE FROM YOUR MOUTH!"

"DO NOT CHEW ON THE DINING ROOM TABLE!"
"WHY ARE YOU THROWING UP?
DID YOU EAT THE MINNIE MOUSE?!"

I ask myself at least twenty times a day, "Why did I adopt
so many animals?" Why did I allow myself to get suckered into
their cute faces and feel sympathetic to the plight of homeless dogs
and cats who needed a loving home? Those same animals - albeit
very cute, homeless animals -have destroyed furniture, eaten
countless items no dog should ingest, and have had countless
"accidents" in our house. They shed hair all over the place, causing
little tumbleweeds of dog hair to blow about the floor. They dig
huge holes in the yard which now resembles the surface of the
moon. They bark and howl at leaves falling off trees and most
anything that moves. They drink my coffee when I am not looking.
They stink, and giving them a bath is akin to trying to dress an
octopus in a button-up shirt. Why, oh why, do I have so many
animals? Six, to be exact: three dogs and three cats. Then, they do
something unexpectedly amazing.

After they have chewed up Minnie Mouse and thrown up
her plastic arms and legs all over the new carpet, they slink onto
the couch where I am sitting. They slide over, put their head into
my lap and look up at me with huge brown eyes full of love and
simple joy. When our three-year-old daughter is playing in the
backyard, they play with her. They crowd around her, and when
she goes down the slide on the swing set, they make sure she
doesn't hit the ground too hard. When she runs across the yard
chasing a butterfly, they break her fall if she trips. When dinner is

over and our gorgeous daughter has thrown most of it onto the floor, they dogs happily lap up every crumb. They follow my daughter to the bathroom as she gets a bubble bath, monitoring us to make sure we don't let her fall under the water or stick anything up her nose. When she cries, they rush to her side and lick her face. They lie next to her, willing her to stop and letting her smash her face into their sides and cry into their fur. They let her hug them with tiny toddler arms that squeeze their necks with surprising strength. They let her dress them up in tiaras, frilly tutus, and even paint their toenails with glittery purple polish. When we are all gone and the house is quiet, they keep watch. If so much as a leaf falls from the tree outside the window, they bark. The neighbors are comforted by the fact that our dogs will alert them to any unusual activity in the area. When my husband is gone—which is frequently, given his military career— they sleep in bed with me, keeping me safe and letting me cry tears of loneliness and sometimes fear into their fur. They snuggle closer to me, licking the tears from my face. I can tell them all my worries, all my fears, and they won't ever repeat a word. They just listen silently, with love and compassion in their big brown eyes. When my husband is having a bad day, perhaps remembering a time in years past when a friend and colleague lost their life in the Hell on Earth that was Iraq, they will lie quietly by his side, understanding that sometimes all you can do is just be there. So, no matter how Minnie Mouses they throw up on my carpet or how many pieces of furniture they destroy, adopting a bunch of animals has brought more blessings into my life than I can count. No matter how frustrated I get with them, or how insane they drive me, they make my life better. My daughter will grow up knowing the love of dogs and of having kindness and compassion for all of God's creatures. I think it is an integral part of childhood, having the love of a dog and experiencing the type of unconditional love only an animal can give you. Animals enrich your life and your soul. I am so very thankful for the ability to have them as a part of our house, and our lives.

"Who teacheth us more than the beasts of the earth, and maketh us wiser than the fowls of heaven? – Job 35:11

Murghi Uncle; 2/25/15

    David Bissette is one of my best friends in the whole world. We have similar tastes in music, movies, and humor. He is a wise grassroots man I sought out many a year ago for his advice on Chunky Junk, a fair trade jewelry company we own that supports our orphanage. I discovered that we are cut from the same cloth. In fact, I think of him now as more of a big brother, more so than any friend I have. He has been to Haiti with me doing building projects for an orphanage. We were even in an epic movie that one will soon not forget. Well, it's hard to forget something you will never see. The movie was a low-budget film that will probably never make the light of day unless you search for it. David is the founder of The Grain Mill of Wake Forest in Wake Forest North Carolina, http://www.grainmill.coop. The Grain Mill of Wake Forest specializes in bulk foods and whole grains, natural salts and sweeteners, and baking supplies. He was the first person I called when God moved me to start Resplendent Farms here at the orphanage. Within three weeks, he was on a plane over to India. Because he was vital in the startup of our chicken farm, the boys started calling him Murghi Uncle, which in India means Chicken Uncle. He is a true friend in the purest sense of the word. I am deeply indebted to David Bissette. His practical love and respect for animals has taught me a lot. I have asked him to write a guest blog for the Animal Awareness Month and he obliged in grand fashion. I hope you enjoy it as much as I have.   Thanks Dave! - Andy

David Bissette's Blog Post:

Several days before Hurricane David wound a path of destruction and havoc through the eastern coast of the United States in 1979, my dad brought home a small flock of chickens. He told me these were special chickens. Rather than laying plain old white or brown eggs, these "Easter Egg" chickens would lay eggs that were blue or green, and sometimes even pink. I thought it was the coolest thing ever.

As a kid, I learned a lot from keeping chickens. Since I was solely responsible for the upkeep of the birds, I had to ensure that my chickens had fresh water and feed, even on the cold days when their water was frozen solid.

Keeping chickens was also my first experience dealing with the sensitive topic of death. Something that my parents didn't explain to me was that there's a reason why everything tastes "just like chicken." It's because everything in the woods seems to enjoy eating them. Raccoons, skunks, snakes, opossums, and the neighbor's dogs all had their eyes on my small flock. One day, I came home from school to find the chicken coop empty. There was nothing there; no hens, no rooster, no feathers. I was completely dumbstruck. I found a very traumatized rooster in a cardboard box in the basement.

Since then, I have had many, many batches of chickens. I learned some valuable lessons from those first birds of mine: kids don't have to be insulated from the way things are. I found out the hard way that chickens are at the bottom of the food pyramid, and death is the natural and inevitable consequence of life. Additionally, I learned that chicken wire is very good at keeping chickens in, but very bad at keeping dogs out.

Thirty-plus years later, the memories of my special chickens is still intact. When Andy Lepper invited me to come to India and Shiloh Orphanage to set up a chicken coop for the boys, I knew I had to do it. One long plane flight and a white-hair inducing cab ride to the city later, Andy, the boys and I were ready to get down to the brass tacks of building a chicken coop with whatever materials we could scrounge.

The first step for the boys was building the enclosure which was a woven fence made from pieces of old bed post and the woody stems from last season's lentil plants. Then the "Murghi Mahal" was constructed of two old bunk beds, a rusted air conditioner cover, some extra scrap lumber, and a piece of donated lexan roofing from a local business owner. Total cost of building our new chicken palace? Less than five American dollars!

Populating it was even easier. After a jaunt through the nearby village, we found a farmer willing to part ways with a rooster "Bada Lal" and two hens, one of which had chicks. We woke the next morning to the sound of cock-a-doodle-doo coming from outside; a familiar sound from my childhood, and one I've missed greatly since moving to the city.

Unfortunately, by the time our chicken coop was completely populated, it was then time for me to return from whence I came. Andy sent me regular updates on the status of the chickens. I think I was nearly as excited as he was about their first eggs, and heartbroken when one of the chicks drowned during a rainstorm. What really excited me was that several of the boys had taken a liking to caring for the chickens. One boy, Mannie, had become a right fine chicken whisperer.

Then came the day when Andy told me about a new breed of chicken he'd been researching; one that could better withstand the dry summer heat in the city and still put on weight. He told me of his plans to purchase hundreds of these birds and raise them not only for eggs and meat for the boys of Shiloh, but for commerce and barter in the community as well.

And lo and behold, if he ain't gone and done it! The orphanage is a regular working farm now. They even grow and grind their own feed for the birds.

I am certainly proud of what's been accomplished at Shiloh, and very grateful that I could be a small part in the much bigger picture of teaching these young men some of the sustaining principles of self sufficiency and life in general. – David Bissette

One of the Greatest Days of My Life

You remember certain days more than others. Some you want to remember, and some you want to forget. I want to forget the many days I learned that someone close to me had passed. In that very moment and day, I wasn't concerned with their eternal security. I was mourning the hole they left in my heart. I was hurting for what was taken from me. I am selfish, and loss hurts. You learn to deal with it, but my initial reaction is always sadness and confusion. I still haven't come to grips with death. Someone once told me to just "get over it. Death is natural and all a part of life." Well, it doesn't feel natural to me for a thirty-five-year-old father and husband to be taken so early. I don't doubt God for a moment, but I just don't understand it. And it feels horrible. Luckily, those days are few and the good far outweighs the bad. The days I want to remember are the ones of joy. I want to remember my special birthdays, and I do. I also remember my wedding day like it happened hours ago. I remember certain days here with our Shiloh boys that I will cherish forever. One day in particular has become the greatest day of my life. It was September 18, 2015. That was the day my wife gave birth to our first son. Four times every second, all around the world, a baby is born. The circumstances surrounding the birth of my son make it the greatest thing to ever happen to me. My feelings are intensified because of the buildup to the birth. That is an epic story all unto itself. You see, my wife and are are not newly married. I am not old, but I sure ain't no spring chicken. I am pushing forty and my wife and I have been married for thirteen years. Not exactly the time to have your first child, but that wasn't by design. We were married in India in 2003 in front of 1,500 orphans. We tried from the beginning to start our family. We tried. And we tried. And. We. Tried. But nothing. Days turned into weeks, weeks into months, months into years. I wasn't exactly young when we were first married, so I thought I was ready. In India, you have kids as soon as you are married. A young couple on our staff had a baby ten months after their wedding day. That is all too common. But we waited. We felt the pressure from our Indian friends and family. They made us feel as if it were a choice for us to wait. There was no choice whatsoever. I have been dreaming of being a father since I was young. I wanted to be the type of father that my father was to me. I wanted to carry on the legacy. I also felt outside pressure even though it was unintentional. I am the only male on my father's side of the family. I have a sister and four female cousins. I felt the burden of carrying on the Lepper name. Laugh all you want at the name, but men of endless integrity and deep convictions have carried this name. It is an honor to be a Lepper. I wear the name like a badge of honor, so naturally I felt the burden of passing it on. It seemed it wasn't meant to be. We went to fertility specialists in the United States and in India. Some couldn't see any problem, but most said there was no chance of getting pregnant. We both were tested and found out that the problem wasn't mine. That broke my heart. I can take the pain of it being my fault, but I just couldn't take it that Susan felt it was her fault. What a helpless feeling! Susan continued to go to various doctors, all having conflicting and somewhat confusing advice. We held out hope that God would heal her and knew that it would take a miracle. I began to shut down and suppress the desire to have my own child. This was about the time we took over leadership of the Shiloh Children's Home. Meeting these boys for the first time filled a void in my heart that I tried to suppress. Very quickly, these kids became more than boys; they became my sons. That was enough, (and still is). Maybe it was the receding of our stress level, or maybe it was because the Shiloh boys made us a Papa and Mommy for the first time, but either way, we fell in love and we had indescribable peace.

But God wasn't finished. He heard our prayer and He was about to answer. Secretly, Susan was still holding out hope. It wasn't like she was hiding, but she had continued to secretly take pregnancy tests holding out hope. On the morning of February 10, at 4 a.m., Susan woke me up by tapping me on the cheek. She kept saying, "I peed! I peed." I congratulated her and asked if I could go back to sleep. "Wake up you idiot! I think I am pregnant!" Through crusty eye boogers, I noticed the pee stick with which she had been tapping me on the cheek. It showed two straight pink lines. I couldn't believe it. I wanted to believe it, but my hope had been wavering for so long. I called my best friend Jason who is a trauma surgeon. He told us that there were no false positives with pregnancy tests, so it was likely true, but encouraged us to go to a doctor for confirmation. Later that day, Susan did just that and it was confirmed. We were going to be parents. I will save the full story for another book, but on September 18, 2015, we welcomed Andrew Michael Lepper Jr. into the world. We decided to call him Micah. It had been decades since we had separately prayed for a child and thirteen years since we started praying together. I still can't believe we have a son!

I want to candidly share this with you — my love for Micah is no greater and no less than it is for our other forty-five boys. It is just different because of how God answered the prayer of our hearts after praying for so long. Likewise, my love for these forty-five boys is different because of how God called us here and made the way possible. I can sit and hold Micah and cry because of how faithful God is. At the same time, I can sit and hold Mark and cry because of the circumstances of why he is here. I love Mark more than words can express. My heart breaks when I think of the mother that abandoned him on our doorsteps. To be able to hold him and to be the only father Mark knows is a responsibility I don't take likely. I actually had a couple of people ask me if we would move back to the United States now that Micah was born. They went on to say now that we had our own child, surely the void was filled in our hearts. Excuse me? We have not sacrificed everything we have ever known to come reduce these orphans to fill a void in our hearts! And we surely wouldn't turn right around and abandon them all over again because we had our own child. Seriously? I just do not understand, and I guess I never will. I have even had adoptive parents tell me that I should have separation between the rest of the orphans and me, Micah, and Susan. Oh really? Is that what people do also with children they have adopted? On one hand, we have left everything we have ever known in the United States. We left our jobs, our homes, our family, and our friends. Not to mention Chick Fil A. We didn't do this to become guardians or dorm parents. We are not an uncle and auntie to the boys. When we left everything, we did it because these boys needed a father and mother. Might I add here that I actually do not feel or believe that we have made a sacrifice of any kind. People may count what we have given up to serve these boys, but to us it is not a loss. When David Livingstone was asked about the sacrifice of leaving England to serve in Africa his response was this, "It is emphatically no sacrifice. Say rather it is a privilege. Anxiety, sickness, suffering, or danger, now and then, with a foregoing of the common conveniences and charities of this life, may make us pause, and cause the spirit to waver, and the soul to sink; but let this only be for a moment. All these are nothing when compared with the glory which shall be revealed in and for us. I never made a sacrifice." And so it is with Andy and Susan Lepper. When it comes to rescuing and serving these orphans, we have never made a single sacrifice. NOT.EVEN.ONE. These kids have been abandoned by every single person they have ever known. I empathize with their families that have left them here because they felt they had nothing to offer. We do have something to offer. And we do have a void in our hearts. But it's a God-shaped hole. That cannot be filled in with any relationship in the world. Wealth can't fill it. Neither came fame or status. This God-shaped hole can be filled by laying our life down to bring glory to God. This is different for everyone. God has called us here not as travelers or missionaries, or buddies for these boys. We are here as Papa and Mommy. No offense intended, but you can have your mission trips. We don't want them. We don't want a trip dedicated to missions. We want a life dedicated to missions. We love, care for, and provide for these boys with every fiber of our being. Some may come and go at no fault of our own. They may grow up and leave or have a family member come and take them back. That doesn't stop them from always being my boys. Your love must not be a reflection of someone's reaction to your love. Your love must be unconditional. It has no strings attached. And love has no motives. I am here because of my deep love for God and these boys, not because I have ulterior motives or any expectations for them. My sincerest prayer is that they become true worshippers, but I will love them regardless of their reaction to my love. Haven't you had relationships where the love was uneven? Maybe you loved someone with a different intensity than they loved you. Maybe you loved them long before that love was reciprocated. I feel that daily. The levels of love shown me from the boys can be as different as extreme hugs and affection from one boy to rejection and apathy from another. I don't love the apathetic child any less than the affectionate one. In fact, it strikes the fire within even hotter to be the love that this boy may have never seen. If you have kids, maybe you can relate to the point that your love for each is equal but not the same. You may love the creativity of one child but the deep thinking of another. Its no greater or less love, it's just displayed differently. Maybe I am utterly naive and no one else will ever get it, but my love for Micah is not greater than my love for these orphans; It is just different.

One of the many reasons I love Micah is because he is the physical embodiment of God's faithfulness. Long ago, I stopped fervently praying for a child and was resigned to the fact that if it was to be then it would happen. I felt that I had prayed enough and that God would either give or He wouldn't. But Susan never stopped praying. God heard her prayer. The funny thing is, as I was too broken to even utter a prayer, Susan was proclaiming bold prayers. Everyone she told laughed at her and mocked her when she said she was praying for a blonde hair, blue eyed baby. Many believed that would never happen because of how dominant her India-ness is. I write to you today about God's answered prayer, not just for a baby, but one that on this very day still has blue eyes and little tufts of blonde hair. It seems to good to be true, but God did it. We have begun joking with baby Micah that the reason it took 13 years for us to have him is because it took that long for God to find a blonde hair blue eyed indian boy with such a sweet heart. He is quite the package. I am unabashedly his biggest fan, but this has to be one of the calmest babies ever. He RARELY ever cries. He is so content and calm. And that is just what we needed. God knew that.

I was reminded this week of the story of Lazarus. God has used it in a special way to speak to me. In case you are not aware of the story, I will keep it simple. Lazarus and Jesus were friends. In fact, people referred to Lazarus as the "one that Jesus loved." Lazarus became very sick and his sisters sent for Jesus. Jesus purposefully waited longer even though He probably wanted to be with His friend. Jesus exact words as found in John 11:4 are, "This sickness will not end in death, but is for the glory of God, so that the Son of God may be glorified through it." After hearing that Lazarus was sick, Jesus waited two more days before he even started His journey. It's not like He was walking down the block. It took Him days to get to Lazarus. In fact, by the time He got there, Lazarus was not only dead, but had been buried for four days. This didn't exactly sit well with Lazarus's sisters even though they loved Jesus. They asked him why he didn't come sooner. Mary said, "If you had been here sooner, my brother would not have died." Everyone was distraught and even Jesus wept. But as the Bible tells us, Jesus stood at the base of the tomb and called Lazarus out. He came to life and walked out of the tomb four days after being put inside the tomb dead. We can glean from this story that Jesus had the power to heal sickness, but instead He choose to heal death. So, my question to you is, Was Jesus late, or was He right on time? Look back to what Jesus said when He found out that Lazarus was sick. He knew that the sickness would lead to death. But He also knew that He would raise Lazarus from that death. The purpose??? "For the Glory of God." If this is the case, then God was not late. Jesus was not late. There was a purpose from the beginning of time for Lazarus. It was meant for his death and life to bring glory to God.

As I read this story, it strangely gave me comfort and peace that I had been missing for MANY years. Even after the birth of Micah, I still questioned God and His timing. Why had HE waited so long? What was the purpose? Quite simply, I can stand before you today and proclaim that God's timing is perfect. He is never late. Why did we have to endure hardship, longing, grief, and pain for thirteen years waiting on the birth of a child? Because of the Glory of God. Plain and simple. No further explanation is needed. No translation will suffice. God was on time even when we didn't comprehend, and Micah's birth and life points to God's Glory. Praise God, great things HE has done. For this main reason, I celebrate the birth of my son, not just because he is an answer to many prayers, but because his birth brought glory to God!

Confession Time

I have a confession to make. I have a favorite donation. How dare I say that in this politically correct world! You can't show favorites! Everyone should get a trophy, right? Well, this isn't exactly like a participation trophy. Let me explain. I will not name names;). We have had donations of up to $5000 from single donors, and everywhere in between, but my favorite donation is $8. I will not say who it's from, but they have been giving to the boys long-term. I have no clue why it's $8. Seems like such a random amount. Maybe that's why it's so intriguing. I have come up with many theories through the years as to why $8. Why not $5 or $10? Why $8? Is it because the donor had exactly that to give the first time they gave and has kept it that way? Is it because that is an equal portion of the tithes and offerings per month? Is the number symbolic? I may never know. Truthfully, I don't want to know. To me it symbolizes three things and that's why it's so memorable:

1. **It's a weird amount**. It's not standard and that's ok. Because I am weird and so are our boys. You may not realize it,

but you are weird too and that's ok. Even the Bible calls us "peculiar people". Weird sticks out. It's memorable and that's what we strive to be for the boys, and pray that that is what they become also.

2. **It's a small amount**. It is our smallest donation. It pales in comparison to some gifts and represents the boys perfectly. They are small and deemed as insignificant. It's like the tortoise and the hare. The unexpected sneaks up on you and ends up surprising you. Our boys are going to surprise this world and do great things. And we like it that way.

3. **Small things can make a big difference**. Over the course of our ministry, this $8 monthly gift keeps coming, month after month. And it keeps adding up. The full amount over the course of more than two years represents many things. It represents the purchase of at least two goats. Or 200 chickens. Or a used motorcycle. Or almost a year of food for one of our boys. Continuity matters. If you don't quit, your life will have more purpose. This is what we teach the boys. Like the widow's mite, success, worship, and giving is not judged by the amount as much as the heart. The world may view our boys as not having much to give, but we know the Bible teaches us that small things given with the heart have lasting impact. Thank you, $8 donor, for teaching us such beautiful lessons.

Acknowledgements

The author would like to thank the following people for their support and encouragement on this journey:

Mary Leaphart, Stephen and Tracie Renfrow, Gareth Johnston, Carole Courcoux-Allyn, Louella Venable, White Creek Baptist Church, Brian and Stephanie Nunes, Jason and Jennifer Johnson, Ron and Joann Schneider, Wesley Denton, The Baptist Church of Beaufort, Laura Swango, Eric Jones, Zachary Kiker, Edward Isbill, Kara Zapata, Scott Koenig, Shirley and Ron Tuttle, Gloria Godwin, Sandra Ivey, Anderson Kinghorn, Dianne McTier, Debbie Parker, Patricia Patterson, Joseph Poveroni, Susan Rodrigue, Teresa Stokes, Rick Tomlinson, Cathy Ragsdale, Catherine Pardue, Pamella Hagan, Martie Collins, Ed and Cindy Duryea, Gloria Godwin, Judy Copeland, Sandra Click, Patsy Brown, Sue Axton, Laure Kline, Erik Peterson, Debbie Merwin, John McAuley, Charles Brabec, Jennifer Greger, Stephanie Lopez Miranda, Jason Hochstein, Randy Bailey, David Bissette, Barbara Nelson, Tatyana Logan, Caleb Atkins, Amy and Benji McCarley, Darcy Boerio, Ashley Osborne, Cheryl Skinner, Luke Mechtly, Shelley Cooper, Kelly Bryant, Chris and Heather Johnson, Jonathan Cook, Al and Sue Lepper, David and April McWhite, Kelly Buchanan, Crystal Perdue, Amanda and Dusty Raines, Gerri Hanson, Nicole Brocato, Leah Wall, Heather Peacock, Ashton Reams, Kimberly Morgan, Arthur Spillers, Heather Hahn, Terra Jones, Kelly Gamble, Chris Leader, Heidi Johnson, Troy High, Nolly Puig, Kimberly Crow, Patrick Henry, Joanna Morrison, Barbara Nelson, Rachel Pawar, Sam Sterling, Marisa Hornish, Danielle Kinney, Chris Fischer, Melissa Deuermeyer, Buckhorn United Methodist Church, Mike and Lynn Lepper, Patricia Myers, Tim and Liz Eaton, Emisenda Long, Melinda Gordon, Charles Whipple, Patricia Lauta, Rebecca Hott, Earl Freeman, JD and Pam Schlieman, Joel and Rebecca Schlieman, Brandon and Kelli Weyand, Fiona Martin, Mark Munson, Jurry Om, Scott Romano, Christine Salm, Johanna Sheridan, Erin Soutter, Cindy Stoutenborough, Sonia Van Soest, Jenifer Frey, David Goold, Kristopher Hamilton, Michael Kottmeier, Laura Krieger, Correen Flatekval, Lauren Courts, Kellie Down, Tania Connolly, Linda Baillargeon, Rea Lorence, Jonathan Surtees, Jennifer Denevan, Jennifer Follestad, Jennifer Gerace, Martha Cazares, Larry Bennett, Cheryl Nichols, Sanabria Deysi, Syed Amiry, Charla Archie, Cheri Olive, Ruth

146

Campbell, Rebecca and Freddie Mercer, Jamie Sheth, Sarah Williams, Lauren Honeycutt, Casey Engen, Rachel Henkel, Loretta and Steve Dukes, Lynda Counts, Cheryl Ward, Alison Newton, Melinda Stembridge, Paul Gainey, Randel Bryan, Charles Cobble, Sidney Bass, Kim, Fortner, Bonnie Horton, Dustin Varn, Christy Waulk, Monica Stout, Ann Sinclair Hamric, Kyle Brown, Valentine Musisi, Mike and Jessica Pope, Jeffrey Roth, Barbara Plotner, Melissa McLean, John Bengier, Julie Joseph, David Loar, David and Wendy Berkhead, Michelle Parnell, Barbara Nelson, Amanda Sealey, Guy and Brandy Spillers, Jon and Tanya Parks, Gloria Spillers, Elizabeth Gibbs, Danielle Boselli, Connie Michael, Calvary Baptist Day School, Concetta Hutton, Thomas Berridge, Jonathan Kerley, Ele Cox, Kady Moore, Jimmy McKenzie, Chris Echterling, Jeff Struecker, Lisa Lacasse, Michael Ferrara, Tamara Dillard, Dr John Keith, Caroline Critzer, Carmel Baptist Church, Jeff and Michelle Dolan, Poplar Springs Drive Baptist Church, Dave Feliciano, Jem Holbrook, Rebecca Duane, Kelley Waller, Casey Kyne, Willy and Victoria Lopez, Dana Kendrick, Crystal Saunders, Mary Holmes, Janet Johnson, Keila Monroe, Stacy Poe, Stephanie Brown, Delila Hodgson, Brian Holbrook, Marcia King, Eric Goodwin, Joseph Cato, Jaime Adams, Sue and Darrell Tuten,

Susan Jennings, Patrick and Dell McGill, Gail High, Cherie Lucas, Melvin Brown, Patti Snyder, Annette Mantooth, Yasemin Yaman, Darrell and Erin Sprinkle, Crystal Saunders, Deborah Thompson, James Cooper, Ron Starley, Valerie Miller, Jerry Blanton, Doug Jinks, Rebekah Wilson, Christine Crafton, Marcia Bailey, Gail Teem, David Townsend, Marguerite Garrett, Linda and Lowell Keen, Susan Dickey, Charles Bush, Orren Bell, Tracy Stembridge, Mike and Joy Connelly, Lisa Harvey, Jim Joyner, Thomas Cecil, Claudia Glasco, Mark Schama, Spring of Hope Christian Church, Oakdale Baptist Church, Hannah Mantooth, Gina Gatlin, Kat Abass, Katie Haney, Caro Robertson, Ethel Johnson, First Baptist Church of Lake Park, Debbie Parker, Marilee Morris, Marilyn Morrow, Lauren Schaefer, Susan Dickey, Duane Hennen, Clayton Porter, Sarah Roux, Ryan Colby, Rebecca Drieling, Teresa Alsing, First Christian Church of Greensburg, Sarah Houser, Penn Mullowney, Clay Duck, Jared Arrowood, Dudley Shoals Baptist Church, Carrie and Roy Whaley, Taylor Meadows, Janice Brogden, Kenneth Wooten, Jared Brogden, Sharyn Sherman, Harold Spence, Bethany Singleton, Ryan Kimbrough, Joel Martin, Kiokee WMU, Braxton and Jess Wynns.

You have read the stories and probably want to get more involved. The easiest and best thing you can do is to sign up to be one of our Project 450 partners. It's only $10 a month but has eternal consequences. Learn more about it at

www.nolongerorphans.org/project_450

If you want to contact us send a message through the website, or to info@nolongerorphans.org